SUNNY SC

A guide to Kihei, Wailea & Makena

Robert Abraham

Arising from crystalline depths, the volcanic cinder cone Puu Olai (360 feet) proudly stands guard over Makena (right) and Little Makena (left) beaches.

TEXT AND DESIGN BY ANGELA KAY KEPLER

Mutual Publishing

John Severson

A colorful windsurfing rig rides a perfect wave.

Copyright ©1992 by Angela Kay Kepler and
Mutual Publishing Company, 1127 11th Ave., Level B
Honolulu, Hawaii 96816 tel (808) 732-1709

Library of Congress Catalog Card No. 92-085477

All photos by Angela Kay Kepler unless otherwise noted.

Front cover photo by Douglas Peebles;
inside cover photo of Maluaka Beach courtesy of
Maui Prince Hotel; inside back cover photo of
Molokini Islet by Douglas Peebles.

Printed in Taiwan

TABLE OF CONTENTS

ACKNOWLEDGEMENTS

One of the most precious aspects of Maui, of all the islands, is not detailed in this book. If one could capture *aloha* in its highest forms—love, genuineness, enthusiasm—I would plead to include such a rare photo...but that inner glow of shared mental, physical and spiritual energy which so enriches island life will unfortunately always remain elusive. To all who have expressed *aloha* to me—outdoor enthusiasts, business contacts, musicians, friends, hotel employees and acquaintances from all walks of life—I return my warm *aloha*. Special gratitude is extended to Inez Ashdown, Liz Beaver, Carol Dawson, Ann Fielding, the late Bernice Flood, Helen James, Joan Judge, Charlie Keau, Kim Marshall, Linda Mather, Joyce Matsumoto, Williet Medeiros, Storrs Olson, Mike Severns, Clyde "Bud" Wagner, Madge Walls, Robert Warzecha, Kolleen Wheeler, Gretchen Williams, Carol Zahorsky, and to the Waiehu Sons for their wonderful music. The U.S. Navy permitted us to visit Kahoolawe and take photographs.

Without my hiking and camping partners—Bob Hobdy, Cameron Kepler, Mary Evanson, John Carothers, members of the Sierra and Mauna Ala Hiking Clubs, U.S. Fish & Wildlife Service, and National Park personnel—the extremities of South Maui would not have been so memorable.

Thanks also to the Four Seasons Resort for accommodation, and to the major "Gold Coast" Resorts and the Wailea Destination Association for their varying kindnesses. These organizations, and many other friends and artists generously allowed me to use their photographs. This includes Ray Mains, the major photographer for Wailea Destination Association. Thanks are extended to Sue Nakamura for the final draft of the map, and to Bonnie Fancher for typing the manuscript. I would also like to thank my children for their good behavior, my brother Howard Brownscombe for his aerial flight, and my husband, Cameron, for his encouragement, ideas, and proofreading.

Me ke aloha pumehana (from the heart with love).

Ed Robinson

The elegant banded prawn (*Stenopus hispidus*), also called barbershop shrimp, is a delicate, spidery denizen of Hawaii's coral reefs.

PREFACE

Maui's "Gold Coast": a dream destination of hundreds of thousands of people each year. Its sweeping golden beaches, velvety golf courses, opulent hotels and spas, valuable art, verdant landscaping, panoramic views and bright-hued coral reefs are widely advertised. However, this beautiful area offers even a greater richness for those with curious minds and discerning eyes.

The second largest of the Hawaiian Islands, Maui's 729 square miles include two mountain masses (10,000-foot Haleakala to the east and 5,788-foot West Maui Mountains) connected by a low-lying isthmus. This book covers the area south of Kahului airport, on through the isthmus (Central Maui) and down the southern shore of Haleakala (South Maui). Its primary focus is Maui's "Gold Coast," a twelve-mile stretch of scalloped, sandy coastline, today a coveted international tourist destination. Also included are two wildlife refuges (Kanaha and Kealia Ponds), Molokini Island, Kahoolawe, and the extensive, uninhabited coastline south of Makena.

Each chapter corresponds to a stretch of road of variable length (see map), covering a wide spectrum of topics: accommodation, art, beaches, birds, climate, culture, dining, entertainment, flowers, geography, geology, Hawaiian mythology, history, hotels, marine biology, shopping, snorkeling and sporting activities.

Central and South Maui provide a study in contrasts: green and brown, rich and poor, humid and dry, calm and windy. Stop frequently, using your senses to their fullest capacity. Fill your visual space with the grandeur of Maui's voluminous skies, focus on the interplay of light and water, imbibe the bounty of island colors and fragrances—and the magic of Maui will uplift you.

Wailea Beach, bathed in dusk's bluish hues.

BENNY + NORMA GORDON
808 879-9314.
2531 SOUTH KIEHI RD.
#A103 KIEHI AKAHI.

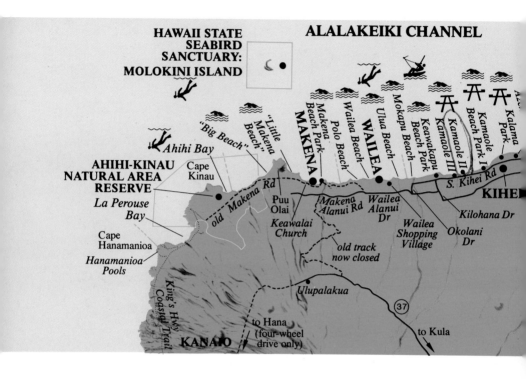

HAWAII STATE
SEABIRD
SANCTUARY:
MOLOKINI ISLAND

ALALAKEIKI CHANNEL

AHIHI-KINAU
NATURAL AREA
RESERVE
*La Perouse
Bay*

Ahihi Bay

"Big Beach"

"Little
Makena
Beach"

MAKENA

Cape
Kinau

Makena
Beach Park

Polo Beach

Wailea Beach

WAILEA

Ulua Beach

Mokapu Beach

Keawakapu
Beach Park

Kamaole III

Kamaole II

Kamaole Beach Park I

Kalama
Beach Park

S. Kihei Rd

KIHEI

Cape
Hanamanioa

*Hanamanioa
Pools*

old Makena Rd

Puu
Olai

*Keawalai
Church*

Makena
Alanui Rd

Wailea
Alanui
Dr

Wailea
Shopping
Village

Kilohana Dr

Okolani
Dr

*King's Hwy
Coastal Trail*

*old track
now closed*

Ulupalakua

(37)

to Hana
(four-wheel
drive only)

to Kula

KANAIO

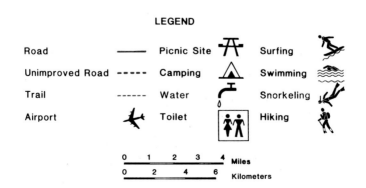

LEGEND

Road	——	Picnic Site	⛩	Surfing		
Unimproved Road	-----	Camping	△	Swimming		
Trail	------	Water		Snorkeling		
Airport	✈	Toilet	🚻	Hiking		

```
0    1    2    3    4   Miles
0      2      4      6   Kilometers
```

6

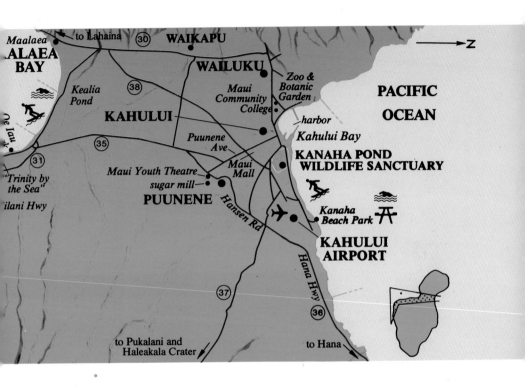

Facts and Figures

- The fifth largest island in Hawaii: 38 miles long by 10 miles wide at its widest point.
- Population 6,500 "friends", a high percentage of Hawaiian extraction.
- Highest sea-cliffs in the world: to 3,500 feet.
- Land area 260 square miles.
- The original home of hula dancing.
- Has a relatively high proportion of its land in natural preserves.
- The site of Hawaii's only Hansen's Disease (leprosy) settlement — now safe to visit.
- Excepting Niihau, the island where Hawaii's ancient spirit is strongest.

CHAPTER I KAHULUI

At dawn on November 26, 1778, Captain James Cook and his crew peered across the Pacific Ocean to a line of small huts scattered along the shore of a broad bay flanked by two impressive mountains. He checked his position: 21 degrees north by 150 degrees west. The island, not marked on any known European chart was called *Mowee* by its natives. The village, from which several hundred canoes and more than 500 swimmers approached him, was Kahului (pron. *ka-hoo-loo-ee*). Cook, needing provisions, bartered nails and pieces of iron for hogs, fowl, cuttlefish, taro and sweet potatoes and other vegetables. Kahului thus became the first center of European commerce on Maui. It has remained a commercial center ever since and is still the primary port of entry for people and commodities from far away. Today, cruise ships arrive in Kahului Harbor every week, and in 1989, two and one-half million people passed through its airport gates. This daily passage of visitors equals half of Kahului's population and would certainly overwhelm it if they stayed. However, the vast majority head for Kihei-Wailea-Makena or Lahaina-Kaanapali-Kapalua, leaving Kahului to the locals.

Kahului has never been a tourist destination. It grew because of its strategic location. By the late 19th century, it had become an important sugar plantation town inhabited primarily by Hawaiians and Orientals, who had been imported to work in the canefields. Hawaii's first railroad connected Kahului and Wailuku and some of its original wooden ties recently became incorporated into West Maui's "Sugar Cane Train."

Early travelers noted that Kahului was dingy and unsanitary. John Musick (in *Hawaii...Our New Possessions*) wrote in 1898 that "the first glance of Kahului is by no means inspiring. A collection of low houses along a beach washed by surf, a railway train...and about two dozen Chinese huts, made up the scene which met our gaze. There was not a single hotel or place where a traveler might rest his weary head.... Kahului as a business center is a failure.... What is worse, there are no white people in the village. One is as much among Orientals in Kahului as if he were in China or Japan. A Chinaman has what he calls a restaurant, but I advise all travelers to avoid Chinese restaurants, unless a white man presides over the institution." In 1900, the entire town was overrun by bubonic plague and had to be burned and rebuilt.

(opposite) Each summer various Buddhist sects (Hongwanji, Jodo) celebrate traditional Japanese **BON DANCES**. Here, lovely ladies dressed in *ukatas* (informal *kimonos*) move to the powerful accompaniment of *taiko* drums as they honor the memories of their ancestors. Rarely observed outside Japan, these colorful, happy festivals are open to the public.

David Davis

After World War I, Harry and Frank Baldwin, descendants of early missionaries, decided to convert Kahului into a "dream city," and it has undergone expansion ever since. Well laid-out, with ample parking, Kahului still has only one main street, Kaahumanu Avenue (Route 36), named after King Kamehameha I's favorite wife. Several shopping centers, a hospital, four hotels (Maui Beach, Hukilau, Maui Palms, Maui Seaside) and several restaurants all lie within close proximity.

Kahului is an excellent place to become acquainted with the diversified lifestyles of Maui's multiracial people. The island's population, as elsewhere in the state, is a constantly changing demographic melting pot. Ethnic backgrounds are approximately: 20 percent Japanese, 26 percent Hawaiian and part-Hawaiian, 25 percent Caucasian (haole), 16 percent Filipino, 11 percent mixed (except part-Hawaiian), and 2 percent other races such as Chinese and Korean.

Most of Maui's communications originate in Kahului. Nine radio stations (four AM and five FM), one daily newspaper, the Maui News plus the weekly South Maui Times and Lahaina Press serve the island. Three national TV networks are represented by four TV stations, ETV and limited cable service. Other radio and TV stations reach Maui from Honolulu, seventy miles (twenty-five minutes by air) away.

BALDWIN BEACH PARK, a long sumptuous stretch of golden sand adjacent to picnic, playing and camping facilities, lies just east of Kahului. Popular with residents, it affords excellent bodysurfing and boogie-boarding for beginners.

Although for centuries Hawaiian outriggers had landed in **KAHULUI BAY**, when King Kamehameha I beached his war canoes here in 1790 he altered Hawaiian history forever. By soundly defeating Maui's defenders at the Battle of Kepaniwai, he conquered Maui, a crucial step in becoming the first chief to rule all the islands. Kahului Bay has since become a highly modified, deep-water harbor witnessing "invasions" of a different nature. Here, the interisland cruise ship *Independence* brings hundreds of visitors weekly to Maui, while fishermen test their luck in the calm waters of Pier 2.

KANAHA BEACH PARK, shoreward of the airport through the rental car area and close to Kahului, is good for novice windsurfing and picnics. Wear footwear on account of the numerous kiawe spines. Here begins the internationally renowned summer event, "Run-to-the-Sun," a gruelling 37-mile supermarathon course which runs from sea level to the top of Haleakala (10,020 feet).

MAUI ZOO AND BOTANICAL GARDENS

Maui Zoological and Botanical Gardens, of dual interest, houses a small assemblage of birds, mammals and reptiles, and a unique collection of native and Polynesian-introduced plants. Though primarily for children, the zoo's endangered birds (*koloa* duck, *nene* goose and Hawaiian Stilt) also lure adults. Notable plants include *wauke*, from which Polynesian tapa (bark cloth) was made, and *koa*, a prized native wood. Photo depicts the large, scented, **OAHU WHITE HIBISCUS** (*Hibiscus arnottianus*), one of Hawaii's showiest native plants, taken in the Koolau Mountains, Oahu, but on display here. To locate the zoo, turn *makai* (toward the ocean) off Kaahumanu Avenue (Route 36) onto Kanaloa Avenue opposite the hospital.

Warren King

(**left**) The **NENE** (*Branta sandwicensis*) is an endemic upland goose bearing obvious kinship with the mainland's Canada Goose. During its evolution, the *nene* forsook the coastal lowlands and marshes, thus adapting to the high lava expanses of Maui and the Big Island. This strange goose is now so comfortable in this arid alpine environment that it can live its entire life without either swimming in, or drinking, water.

PUUNENE

Puunene village, just beyond the outskirts of Kahului, is barely more than a sugar mill and museum, a spattering of homes, a tiny Post Office and the offices of Hawaiian Commercial and Sugar Company (HC&S). Today it is a mere skeleton of a once-prosperous sugar-plantation town that flourished for decades. Most "company towns" have faded into oblivion, but the East Maui Irrigation Company's town of Kailua along Maui's Hana Highway still lives.

During the sugar industry's infancy, many immigrants were brought to work in Hawaii from all over the world. The greatest numbers came from Asia. From 1852 onwards, hundreds of thousands of laborers from the Philippines, China, Japan, Puerto Rico, Portugal, Korea, and the United States immigrated. For them, the opportunities to work and provide education for their children were gifts from Providence. Most remained, their descendants intermingling to establish the unique ethnic mix of races that comprises Hawaii's population today. If you enjoy the physical beauty of Hawaii's men, women, and children, then, historically speaking, you have the sugar industry to thank for it!

(*below*) A few picturesque **PUUNENE HOMES** of sugar employees still survive, but for how long? This one disappeared in the late 80s, but will long be remembered, since drivers enjoyed its rambling garden as they waited at the Kihei intersection or turned to park at the old Maui Youth Theatre.

A brilliant rainbow arches northward from Puunene town across a **SEA OF SUGAR CANE** that carpets Maui's isthmus and the lower flanks of Haleakala. Hawaii's thirteen sugar companies grow approximately one million tons of sugar annually, about seventeen percent of the entire U.S. sugar production. *Please remember that driving on cane roads is prohibited.* Prior to harvesting, portions of sugar cane fields are blocked off and burned. These quick, searing **CANE FIRES** dispense with tons of organic debris that have accumulated during the two-year growth period. When mature, cane stalks contain approximately seventy-five percent water; thus, the fire affects their sugar content only minimally.

John Severson

(left) Sugar growing commenced on Maui around 1850. In 1882, the lack of sufficient water, labor shortages and financial difficulties made survival difficult and eventually led to a merger of fourteen small companies into one. At this time, HC&S emerged to dominate sugar production on Maui and continues to do so today. These **HC&S OFFICES**, adjacent to the mill, are neatly landscaped with palms, spacious lawns and shade trees.

(center) Puunene, whose name means "goose hill," boasts an excellent Alexander & Baldwin **SUGAR MUSEUM**, including a restored locomotive from the 1800s. The exhibits pay tribute to this agricultural industry which greatly influenced the evolution of the social, demographic, cultural and business fabric of contemporary Hawaii.

(below) **LADIES** in the sugar fields. Face scarves are necessary, as heavy machinery and constant winds create very dusty conditions.

The **PUUNENE SUGAR MILL'S** tall striped smokestacks are Central Maui's most prominent man-made feature. This complex factory, Maui's largest, operates twenty-four hours a day for most of the year and burns cane wastes (bagasse) for fuel to generate electrical power. Its maze of motors, pumps, spouts, conduits, cleaners, shredders, boilers, pans and evaporators is geared to undertaking a seemingly simple task: that of converting the sap of sugar cane, a giant grass, into crystals of raw sugar. Raw sugar is available from markets and in tiny brown packets on restaurant tables. Its pale tan, translucent crystals are larger, more angular and tastier than those of white sugar, and because of their higher molasses content, are richer in vitamins and minerals. The conversion of raw to white sugar takes place in California.

(*bottom*) A shady tunnel of **MONKEYPODS** (*Samanea saman*) and **EARPODS** (*Enterolobium cyclocarpum*) flanking Puunene Avenue extend the village's arbor-like atmosphere.

WILDLIFE REFUGES: KANAHA AND KEALIA PONDS

Two of the state's primary wetlands lie within the geographic area covered by this book. Both provide nesting, feeding and "loafing" areas necessary for the survival of migratory and endangered resident birds. (*top*) **KANAHA WILDLIFE SANCTUARY** (pron. *ka-nah-hah*), a series of ponds and *kiawe* forest covering 143 acres, lies *makai* (seaward) of the road as you drive from Kahului airport towards town. Adjacent to Route 36 is a small observation pavilion. Mounded islets have been provided for stilt nests, and a fence prohibits dogs and mongooses from devouring their young. (*bottom*) **KEALIA POND** (pron. *kay-ah-lee-ah*), a larger, amorphous area with fluctuating water levels lying on the opposite side of Maui's isthmus from Kanaha, embraces approximately 500 acres. After lengthy negotiations, in 1992 Kealia was finally incorporated into the US Fish and Wildlife Service Wildlife Refuge System.

Cameron Kepler

17

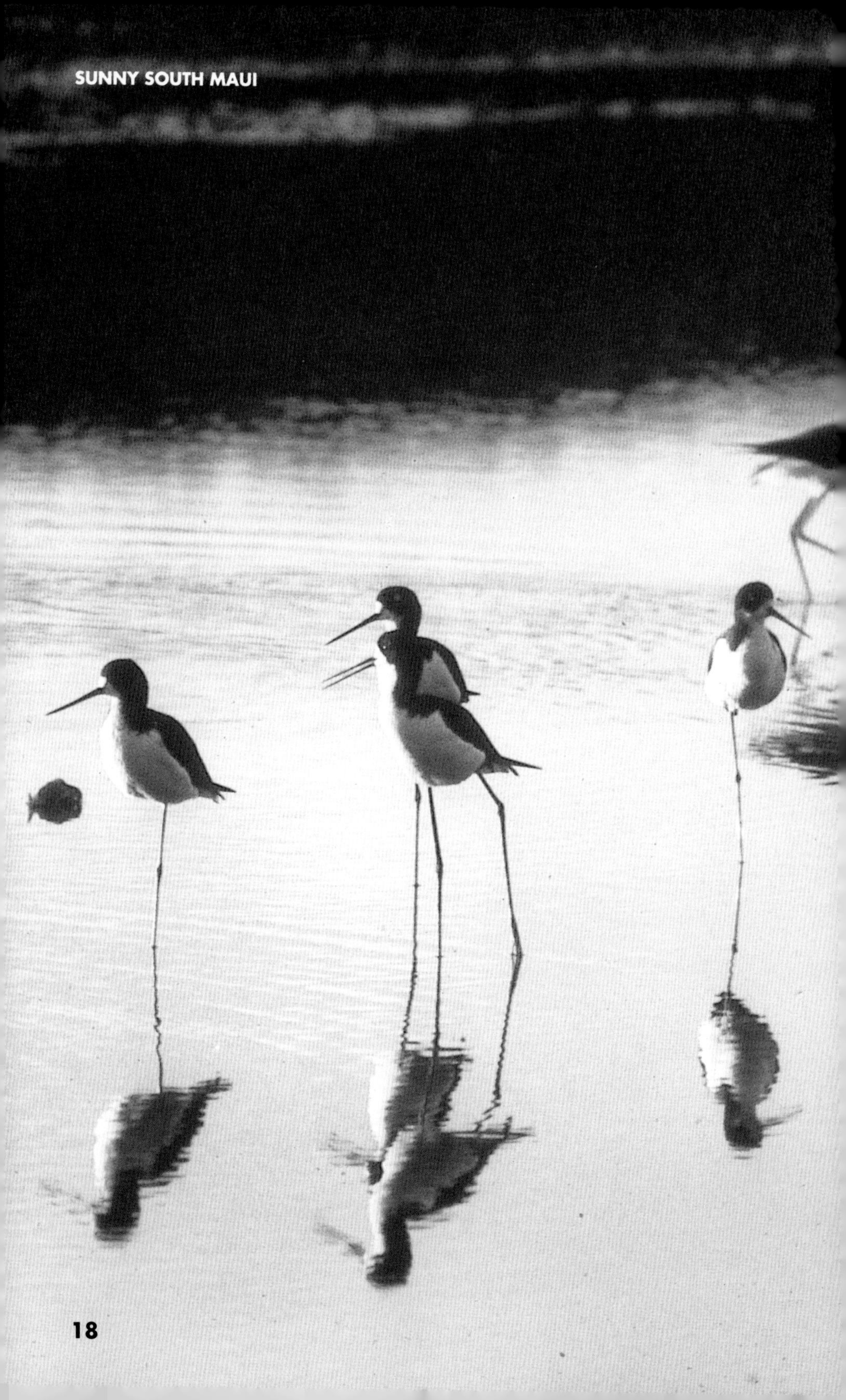

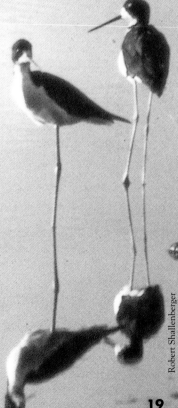

Robert Shallenberger

Planeloads of visitors stream into Hawaii's airports daily, with much of the state's economy, prime land and entertainment focusing upon their temporary welfare. There is, however, another class of transient visitors who are beneficial even though they attract no publicity. They similarly descend annually on island terrain by the thousands. No one checks their "baggage" or tabulates their total numbers, and few appreciate their remarkable navigational skills or the vast hazardous distances they have traversed. Instead of reclining in comfort while traveling, feasting on tasty dinners washed down with champagne, they use their own wings to fly 2,400 miles from Alaska to Hawaii, rarely stopping for a bite to eat. So efficient is their body metabolism that a biologist once calculated that one nine-inch species utilized *less than one ounce of fat* during its entire four-day flight!

These visitors are migrant shorebirds, thirty-five species in all. As with human visitors, they arrive unexpectedly or with such regularity that you can practically predict their arrival date. Certain individuals return to precisely the same sandy cove or backyard that they preferred in previous years. Hunting is illegal.

The four species most commonly encountered, and which may migrate together, are: Lesser Golden-Plover (*kolea*), Wandering Tattler (*ulili*), Ruddy Turnstone (*akekeke*) and Sanderling (*hunakai*). At least three have Hawaiian songs written about them. All live dual lives: "at home" on the arctic tundra where they raise their families in summer, and "on winter vacation" in the equable climates of Pacific islands. Except for these shorebirds, Hawaii is home to only a few coastal and marsh-loving birds. This often surprises mainlanders who expect a more varied and abundant bird life.

Pelicans and gulls flying offshore, skies filled with squawking ducks, and branches weighted down with roosting herons—Hawaii is not the place for these particular natural spectacles. This is due to its geographic isolation; the predatory habits of dogs, cats and mongooses; and the ever-increasing loss of wetland habitats.

(previous pages) The **HAWAIIAN STILT** or *aeo* (*Himantopus mexicanus knudseni*) is an endangered form of the North American Black-necked Stilt. These handsome, slender, black-and-white wading birds sport elongated pink legs, hence the common name "stilts." Though hunted as game until 1941, they are now protected, their statewide population fluctuating around 1,400 individuals. Approximately forty percent of these live on Maui. They are not migratory, and may be observed all year.

Kilauea National Wildlife Refuge

It is undoubtedly surprising to hunters that coots, instead of being practically "vermin," are endangered in Hawaii. The slate gray, duck-like **HAWAIIAN COOTS** (*Fulica americana alai*) were popular food in old Hawaii and were known as *alae keokeo* or "white mudhen." They were simple to catch: one merely chased and pelted them with stones.

Robert Shallenberger

The **BLACK-CROWNED NIGHT-HERON** (*Nycticorax nycticorax*) is one of Hawaii's largest resident birds, its handsome blue-gray body standing two feet high. So intently does it stalk its prey of fish, mice, frogs, insects, the Hawaiians, who called it *aukuu*, likened its behavior to that of a spy.

21

David Boynton.

Common on lawns, beaches and in upland pastures, the *kolea* or **LESSER GOLDEN-PLOVER** (*Pluvialis fulva*) is a small shorebird seven inches tall. Photo shows its handsome breeding plumage: black-and-white frontal patterning and gold-spangled body. This bird (sexes are identical) is about to fly to Alaska, where it will court, mate and raise its family on the arctic tundra. Most plovers are absent from Hawaii between May and August. During the rest of the year, their plumage is a plain mottled golden-brown.

The ancient Hawaiians regarded the *kolea* with a mixture of fear and respect. It was something of a god to them, as its habits—plumage changes, sudden disappearances and seeming lack of nests—were puzzling. However, when the Hawaiians were informed of the biological facts, they invented a clever saying: *The* haole *(foreigner) is like a* kolea—*he spends the winter in Hawaii and returns in fattened condition to the coast of America.*

Maalaea Bay, **KEALIA POND (left center)**, the **KIHEI COAST** and the cloud shrouded mass of Haleakala are viewed from a grassy ridge 3,000 feet above Maalaea (pron. *ma-a-lie-ah*). When rainfall is scarce and water levels low, as pictured, some waterbirds fly to other islands to feed and nest. In winter this is a "hot-spot" for migratory ducks and shorebirds, also attracting rare vagrants (i.e., lost birds) such as mainland gulls, terns and ospreys. The Sierra Club holds an annual February bird-watching walk. To reach Kealia, drive to Kihei via Route 350, then turn north on Route 31.

Abundant on all islands except Kauai, the weasel-like, **SMALL INDIAN MONGOOSE** (*Herpestes auropunctatus*) slinks along roadside grasses, often darting across roads. After their introduction in the 1880s, the Hawaiians named them *iole-manakuku*, the "rat-mongoose." Brought here to control large rat infestations in sugar fields, the mongoose's introduction was a disaster: it is active during daylight while its supposed prey, rats, emerge primarily at night! Their voracious predatory habits practically exterminated Hawaii's ground-nesting birds, transmitted diseases and caused havoc in chicken farms. Perhaps their only saving grace is that they also eat cockroaches.

U.S. Fish & Wildlife Service/Dann Espy

23

CHAPTER II KIHEI

A drive through Maui's "Gold Coast" until the 1960s was a quiet ramble through dry forests of *kiawe* flanking a seemingly endless array of lovely golden beaches such as Kamaole Beach Park II (*below*). The land lay empty and unwanted. By the early 1970s, a plethora of condominiums, apartment complexes, budget hotels and residences had sprung up with remarkable speed. Development still continues, spreading inland and southward.

Kihei (pron. *kee-hay*), the first resort area to emerge, was the product of many developers, in contrast to the master-planned resorts of Wailea, Makena and Kaanapali and Kapalua (West Maui). Despite this, Kihei (population 16,000) remains immensely popular. Its gardens burst with tropical verdure, the beach is only a stone's throw away, and tranquility may still be found. This section of the "Gold Coast" is especially favored by Canadians; several condominiums offer toll-free phone service to Canada as well as to the U.S. mainland.

Kihei, whose name means "cape," is perfect for the budget-conscious vacationer who is unconcerned with world-class luxury. The vacation homes here are beautiful (some are luxurious) and are sufficiently gratifying for most people, but if you want total pampering, a higher quality solitude, and all-round sensuous pleasure on this end of Maui, keep driving.

Many fine restaurants, *luau* (Hawaiian feasts), shopping, snorkeling, sailing, whale-watching, SCUBA diving and windsurfing are available. Equipment for water-related sports can be rented from the Ocean Activities Center, dive shops and many resorts. As Kihei is both a residential and resort area, basic services (fast foods, gasoline, fresh produce, doctors, banks, etc.) are close.

Weather is summery—hot, dry and windy, with less than ten inches of rain per year. Temperatures average 71°F to 78 °F with extremes ranging from 49°F to 98°F. Nights and early mornings are warm and gently breezy, but stiff winds pick up during late morning. Beaches are best enjoyed before 11 a.m.

To reach Kihei, drive from Kahului via Route 350 (eight miles) and either take Route 31 (Piilani Highway) south—an inland road that parallels the coast—or the coastal route through the heart of Kihei on South Kihei Road (see map).

A striking orchid tree (Bauhinia monandra) frames the seaside condo, Kauhale Makai, the "Village by the Sea."

KIHEI   BEACHES

Beaches make Kihei...Kihei *is* its beaches. Whichever way you put it, people—residents and an increasing number of visitors—have always come to Kihei for its sun and sand. In contrast to Wailea and Makena, which have discrete sandy coves, most of Kihei is one continuous strip of beach. Natural rocky points and man-made breakwaters excepted, the entire coast is basically sand of varying color and quality. The golden sugary beaches are closest to Wailea. Kihei's entire shoreline experiences occasional *kona* (southern) storms, generally a winter phenomenon. These have eroded the beaches so that fences and sand-binding plants are now necessary for dune stabilization. *Please walk on established tracks.*

Up till 1952, before Maalaea Boat Harbor was built, interisland shipping boats, fishing vessels and pleasure craft landed at a 200-foot-long wharf on Mai Poina Oe Iau ("forget-me-not") Beach **(below).**

Brightly painted outrigger canoes are common. Canoeing in the old Hawaiian style, to which these calm leeward shores are well suited, is both a hobby and competitive sport.

In a cove at the southern end of Mai Poina Park, opposite the Maui Lu Hotel, is a totem pole **MONUMENT** to Captain George Vancouver, erected by Canadians. Vancouver, who arrived in Hawaii only 14 years after Captain Cook, sailed along Maui's south coast in 1793 and briefly landed here before eventually anchoring off Lahaina. One totem pole proudly announces that it was "the first totem pole to fly the Pacific."

Kihei's most popular beach parks, Kalama and Kamaole I, II and III, stretch southward from the Town Center for about a mile. These wide stretches of sugary sand, illustrated here by **KAMAOLE II**, are backed by lawns, shade trees, restrooms, showers, barbecue grills, and picnic tables. Kamaole III also has a children's playground and ample parking. Kalama Park, the largest, includes tennis courts, soccer and baseball fields, a volleyball/basketball court, and pavilions.

The tree with delicate foliage is **KIAWE** (*Prosopis pallida*), a native of Peru which is ubiquitous in lowland Hawaii, particularly in dry areas. Your first encounter with it may well be a sharp pain in your foot. Its twigs, shed all year, are covered with piercing spines. *Always wear footwear when approaching beaches where* kiawe *is present.* Its spines, up to one-half-inch long, can pierce skin, plastic, leather and even car tires. Despite this drawback, *kiawe* is attractive when well watered, and useful, too. Its honey, available from most markets, is tasty; and steaks and seafood broiled over its charcoal (sometimes called mesquite) are scrumptious. Hawaii's "mesquite" is different from, but closely related to, the mesquite in the deserts of the Southwest U.S.

GHOST CRABS or *ohiki* (*Ocypode ceratopthalma*) scurry sideways across the sand or busily construct curved burrows. Though somewhat shy, they typically scrutinize you with their long-stalked eyes between bouts of feeding at the water's edge. Their pincers can draw blood, so if you or your children wish to dig a crab from its burrow, approach it from behind and grab the body as far back as possible. Please release the crab when you have finished looking at it. So few crabs live to maturity on populated beaches that they average half the size of their brothers on remote beaches.

KAMAOLE III is by far the most popular of Kihei's beaches, even though it is fairly small and discrete. Extensive lawns, ample parking, shade, and perhaps family traditions all contribute to its frequent visitation.

(left) Adjoining Wailea, at the southern end of Kihei, is one of Maui's most superb beaches, KEAWAKAPU (pron. "kay-ahv-ah-kah-poo"). This half-mile golden strand is home to several resorts and condos. In center photo is the Mana Kai Condominium: "Spirit of the Sea." Snorkeling is best in front of this resort, where fish are quite tame. An artificial reef installed in 1962 made from fifty car bodies, 400 yards offshore at a depth of eighty feet, has increased both their numbers and diversity.

"GOLD COAST" BIRDS

During the 19th century, people moving to Hawaii to settle were disturbed at the lack of bird life in the countryside and around their homes. Exotic birds were encouraged so much that since 1850 almost 150 species of birds (game and non-game) have been released in the islands, about 30 of which have survived. These introduced birds have completely replaced Hawaii's native birds in the lowlands and many upland areas. The major reason is that exotic species of birds carry pox and avian malaria, diseases to which Hawaii's unique native birds have no natural immunity. Around a dozen exotic land bird species are easily spotted in the Kihei-to-Makena area.

Cameron Kepler

(*left*) One of Maui's commonest birds, certainly the noisiest, is the **COMMON MYNAH** (*Acridotheres tristis*). Its dark brown body and white wing patches are conspicuous, particularly during flight. Originally from India, mynahs were introduced last century to control insect pests in canefields.

Timothy Burr

(*above*) During winter, Kihei's numerous coral trees (*Erythrina* spp.), attract attention. Clusters of crimson sweet-pea like flowers, several inches long, burst from its bare branches. A **HOUSE SPARROW** (*Passer domesticus*) pecks for insects and/or nectar. Other common birds such as Northern Cardinals, Japanese White-eyes and Common Mynahs also utilize this food source. Although Hawaii does have a native coral tree (*wiliwili*) which once thrived here, the ornamentals in urban and resort areas hail from tropical America and other Pacific islands.

Howard Hunt

Cameron Kepler

(*above*) Throughout South Maui the high-pitched coos of the **SPOTTED DOVE** (*Streptopelia chinensis*) and **ZEBRA DOVE** (*Geopelia striata*, *left*) may be heard. (The latter calls are of higher pitch and greater rapidity than the former.) Mynahs and doves, spreaders of avian diseases, have also dispersed lantana, a prickly weed cursed by ranchers.

Timothy Burr

(*left*) It may be a surprise to hear **NORTHERN MOCKINGBIRDS** (*Mimus polyglottos*) on Maui, but they have been here since the early 1930s. If they sound slightly different to the one in your background at home they are only living up to their scientific name, which means "the many-tongued mimic."

31

David Boynton

Timothy Burr

(*top*) No nocturnal recluse, Hawaii's own Short-eared Owl or **PUEO** (*Asio flammeus sandwichensis*) typically flies over open areas during the day. (*center left*) Male **NORTH-ERN CARDINALS** (*Cardinalis cardinalis*) and their mates (*center right*) prefer bushes, whereas the **WARBLING SILVERBILL** (*Lonchura malabarica*) forms small, fast-flying flocks in the *kiawe* scrublands (*bottom*).

CONDOMINIUMS

The condominium (condo for short) is a modern elaboration of a house rental. The living space may be temporary or relatively permanent, a simple studio apartment in a multi-storied complex, or a charming home within a duplex. Condominiums are not usually set up by a single owner or corporation, but by limited partnerships of investors who possess proprietary rights to one or more units. All owners share in the maintenance and landscaping costs of the complex, thus all common areas are held jointly.

The visitor rents a living unit from the management just as he or she would rent a hotel room. Condos are particularly favored by groups or families, as they are complete apartments with a variable number of bedrooms and bathrooms. Cooking facilities include every conceivable option from a basic refrigerator and stove to the all-American dream kitchen sporting a dishwasher, microwave, grill, wet bar, ice- and coffeemaker, garbage disposal and telephone.

Hawaii has the largest number of condo units in the nation, and Maui is second to Oahu in the state. Some are plain rectangular apartment blocks, while others are more creative, maximizing ocean, garden or mountain views for each guest. Amenities include adult and children's swimming pools, air conditioning, golf and putting greens, weightlifting and recreation rooms, sauna/Jacuzzis, barbecues, shuffleboard, tennis, private washing machines and dryers, volleyball, daily maid service and so on. Some house restaurants and grocery stores. Special services include complimentary airport pickup and return, rental car, starter grocery package, guest signing privileges at certain restaurants, and personally tailored "vacation packages."

Kihei offers two price ranges for one-bedroom/one-bathroom rental units that accommodate up to four people. The "regular season" is mid-April to mid-December. Prices are higher for larger units and during "peak season," mid-December to mid-April.

(*above*) Because Kihei is primarily a region of condos, we included the **MAUI LU RESORT** in this section. Built in the 1950s, it was Kihei's sole hotel for years. The lush, 28-acre grounds, Micronesian-style longhouse, weekly *luau*, Polynesian employees, unsophisticated elegance and moderately priced villas contribute to its old-fashioned ambience. The management takes pride in its *ohana* spirit—a "bond of extended family togetherness that brings guest and employee together to share in the warmth of old Hawaii."

Nestled within the Maui Lu's rambling gardens sit individually landscaped **VILLAS** painted in the same shade of green as rural Hawaiian homes of bygone days. The resort owns a sandy cove at the south end of Mai Poina Park, location of the Vancouver Monument. This hotel, cool but tropical, is arbored with tall coconut palms (*left*), that shade the entrance, villas, *imu* (underground oven), and swimming pool sculpted in the shape of the island of Maui.

Colony Hotels & Resorts

(*above*) Opposite Kamaole III Beach Park lies the 15-acre tropical estate of **KAMAOLE SANDS**. Of mid-price range, this condo specializes in luxury kitchens, tennis courts and delightful views. The central garden contains fountains and a meandering stream.

(*left*) Located on eight tastefully landscaped waterfront acres, the **LUANA KAI** lives up to its Hawaiian name: "to live in comfort and leisure beside the beach, amidst pleasant surroundings and associates." Specialties include a putting green, tennis courts and outdoor whirlpool.

(*right*) **KIHEI RESORT**, in the low price range, utilizes its limited space well with neat, private gardens.

(*top*) The renovated ruins of the David Malo Memorial Church, built in 1853, are known as **TRINITY-BY-THE-SEA**. This delightful open-air chapel is dedicated to the memory of an early Hawaiian scholar who authored a classic treatise on island customs entitled *Hawaiian Antiquities*. The original building, fifty-five feet long and twenty-two feet wide, was constructed of coral and stone cemented with lime. For over a century the church was forgotten until its recent refurbishing by the Episcopals. Worshippers of every denomination are welcome at the regular 9 a.m. Sunday services. To reach it, take the second left south of the Maui Lu.

(*above*) Catholic churches in Hawaii often decorate the Virgin Mary with fresh leis. Pictured is **ST. THERESA'S CHURCH** at the corner of South Kihei Road and Lipoa Street.

(*left*) Although the "Gold Coast" appears lush, it is actually a natural desert. Note the **DRY VEGETATION** along highways. To maintain tropical verdure, almost *ten million gallons of water daily* are shunted from streams and underground aquifers from Central and West Maui. From these limited sources also comes water for much of the islands' irrigation and domestic needs. Residents, visitors and developers are requested to be aware that Maui is a small island with renewable, but not inexhaustible, water resources. *Please conserve water wherever possible and do not litter.* Be especially careful with cigarette stubs.

(*center*) **FRESH FISH** are specialties on Maui. (Consult the beach guides, A *Taste of Maui,* and other free literature for specific restaurants.) Pictured at the top is *ulua,* one of the several types of tasty jackfish gleaned from Maui's waters. Inhabiting shorelines, *ulua* (*Caranx sexfasciatus*) have compressed, silvery bodies. They are fast swimmers who rapaciously hunt smaller fish and crustaceans. At the bottom is an *onaga* or pink snapper (*Etelis carbunculus*), which also has delicious, flaky meat.

(*bottom*) Although many shopping centers have sprung up in Kihei recently, **AZEKA PLACE** is special to *kamaaina* (old-timers). As Harry Hasegawa is a tradition in Hana, Bill Azeka is a tradition in Kihei. Until the early 1980s, Azeka's was a simple country store, but despite its recent expansion Mauians still claim that Azeka's take-out marinated short ribs cannot be beat.

CHAPTER III MOLOKINI ISLAND

Arising from a royal blue ocean in an almost perfect crescent, picturesque Molokini (meaning "many ties") sits three miles offshore from Wailea and Makena. A volcanic islet, it is most noted for its coral reefs, tame fish, crystalline waters, superb views of neighbor islands, and cruising whales.

A visit to this partly submerged crater transports us back through timeless eras which embrace the timeless eras of geological and biological evolution, as well as the last few centuries of Hawaiian mythology and present-day happenings. Together they weave a continuum that incorporates fiery lava outpourings, animal and plant adaptation, human beliefs, warfare, conservation and tourism.

From a geological point of view, Molokini, 120 feet high, lies in a chain of relatively recent cinder cones (puu) which extends down Haleakala's southwest flanks, bearing witness to the mountain's most recent volcanic activity. Puu Olai ("earthquake hill"), a 363-foot-high dome on the same rift, is a notable feature of the Wailea-Makena coastline.

In former times such natural phenomena were explained differently: Pele, the goddess of fire, had a dream lover whose name was Lohiau. This man lived at Maalaea and married a *moo*, a large legendary lizard. Pele became so jealous of Lohiau's wife that she chopped her in half. Her head became Molokini and her tail, Puu Olai. Others say that Maui is a woman and Molokini is her *piko* (navel).

The historical land-use of this tiny ash-cone is unusual, but not exceptional, in Hawaii. Around 1900, rabbits were introduced. They lasted until the drought of the 1970s, by which time they had eaten practically every plant on the island. During World War II, the U.S. Navy strafed Molokini. Bombardment was extensive: bullets still protrude from the islet's cliffs, and bomb craters and metal

Ocean Activities Center

Ocean Activities Center

This milletseed butterflyfish (Chaetodon miliaris) has several look-alike relatives.

(*above*) Molokini crater's inner walls sweep grandly upwards to an overhung **JAGGED RIDGELINE.** Ten thousand-foot Haleakala, with Maui's "Gold Coast" dwarfed at its base, looms skyward three miles distant.

fragments dot its terrain. Both environmental "bombshells"—rabbits and military explosives—adversely affected Molokini's marine life, plants and seabirds. In addition, the severe winter storm of 1980 destroyed part of the reef.

Today, in recognition of the island's underwater and terrestrial resources, Molokini is both a Marine Life Conservation District and a State Seabird Sanctuary. Landing is prohibited for three reasons: first, its inner walls are steep, crumbly and honeycombed with over 1,500 fragile seabird burrows (for much of the year, these thin-walled burrows contain eggs, chicks or adults). Second, past military practice has littered the island with debris, some of which may still be unexploded. Third, walking around is difficult, unsafe, and illegal.

Boats must return to Maui before noon because Molokini is daily buffeted by conflicting winds from the north, south and west. Ocean currents surrounding it can be rough and complex. In general, mornings are calm and afternoons very windy.

Enroute to and from Molokini, watch the colors, patterns and moods of sea and sky. Maybe a half-dozen flying fish will unexpectedly skim the water's surface—or a seabird may suddenly swoop down and snap up an unsuspecting fish—or perhaps a porpoise will peer up at you with humanoid eyes then arch gracefully beneath your boat—or a whale may surface right under your nose. You never know. You may see only choppy seas and gray clouds, but whatever the experience, it will be memorable.

Cameron Kepler

(left) The tiny islet's **outer SEA-CLIFFS**, pocked with weathered holes and partly skirted by a wave-cut beach, rise to 120 feet. Six miles away is Kahoolawe, whose high escarpments are also constantly bathed by erosive waves.

(center) Horseshoe-shaped **MOLOKINI** is a popular snorkeling and SCUBA diving destination. The navigational light, installed in 1946, is maintained by the U.S. Coast Guard operating out of Maalaea Harbor, north of Kihei.

Every morning (except during storms), **CHARTER BOATS** wend their way across Alalakeiki Channel to snorkel at Molokini. They originate from Maalaea, Wailea and Makena in South Maui; and Lahaina and Kaanapali in West Maui. Boats provide breakfast, lunch, beverages, underwater gear, instructions and plenty of joviality. Take a windbreaker and sunglasses.

A crescent "moon" highlights the silvery channel, Alalakeiki.

CORAL REEFS

Coral reefs are delicately balanced, complex marine communities that are best developed in the world's warm ocean shallows where food and light are abundant. Each reef may be likened to a miniature, submerged New York City. Its building units are composed of densely packed apartment/condominium complexes of different shapes and sizes. These "condos" have been built by the master builders, corals, which are colonies of tiny animals, and calcareous algae, simple plants containing calcium. As time progresses, algae and corals both add more "rooms" and cement to the existing structures.

The reef "tenants," who enjoy a variety of lifestyles, know where they belong, where the tastiest food morsels may be gleaned, what the community hazards are, and how to avoid them. Many hide during daylight hours and venture out cautiously at night when it is safer. Living within a coral reef may seem idyllic, but it is very easy to become someone else's dinner. "Condo" occupants may be tiny crabs, who help with excavation; fish, who live in passageways; sea-worms, who stretch out their sticky, spaghetti-like tentacles to catch food from a stationary position; and octopi, who are quite mobile. Shrimps, lobsters, starfish, sponges and sea-urchins also occupy these coral tenements.

On first exposure to a reef, most people are attracted to its gaudy fish. Rightly so. However, many invertebrates (animals without backbones) are equally fascinating, but it takes time and expanding awareness to become acquainted with them.

Enjoy Hawaii's reefs and rocky points for their individuality. Their quality varies, and because sediments, winds and surf create turbulence, even the best snorkeling locations may sometimes have murky waters. Remember that although Maui may seem like the tropics (especially if you dug your way out of two feet of snow to catch your plane here), at this latitude (21°N) coral growths are not as luxuriant, as colorful, nor as diverse as reefs that lie closer to the equator such as Fiji or the Great Barrier Reef. Molokini, with clear waters, forty-three species of fish (including manta rays and the harmless white-tipped shark) is as good as Maui can offer. However, if you cannot get there, do not despair. Other good snorkeling spots are Black Rock (Kaanapali), Ulua and Keawakapu beaches (Wailea), and the Ahihi-Kinau Bay Natural Area Reserve (Makena). South Maui's waters are particularly clear because of minimal runoff and pollution.

Ed Robinson

Ed Robinson

Ann Fielding

(*opposite*) A large male **REDLIP PARROTFISH** or *uhu* (*Scarus rubroviolaceus*) such as this crunches down so much coral in a year it manufactures a ton of sand! (*above*) **BLUE-LINED SNAPPERS** or *taape* (*Lutjanus kasmira*) streak over a knobby colony of finger coral (*Porites compressa*). (*below*) A large **SCRAWLED FILEFISH** (*Alutera scriptus*), sports iridescent blue "scribblings" and whiskbroom-like tail as diagnostic features.

43

Ed Robinson

Ed Robinson

(*above*) The **SADDLE WRASSE** (*Thalassoma duperreyi*), one of Hawaii's commonest reef fish, may be your first identified fish. It is characterized by a jaunty purple-blue head and orange band ("saddle") around its green body. Its scientific name commemorates a French ichthyologist who visited Maui in 1819. Wrasses are well known for their bright colors and unique style of swimming—a sort of "rowing" motion using their front (pectoral) fins. Known to the people of old as *hinalea*, wrasses were kept in ponds and used in religious ceremonies.

(*opposite*) Butterflyfishes (*kikakapu*) epitomize coral reefs. They emblazon shallow waters and atoll lagoons with their bold patterns and colors; two-dimensional, practically circular bodies; "kissing mouths;" and enviable agility. The **RACCOON BUT-TERFLY FISH** (*Chaetodon lunula*) sports a facial mask resembling that of a raccoon. A flamboyant fish which often travels in small schools, it illustrates one of Nature's clever camouflage strategies. Notice how its color patterns break up the body contours. If you were a predator you might assume that the fish's eye was that black spot close to its tail. What a surprise to plan your attack and suddenly find your dinner scooting off in another direction! A "false eye" is one of the many ways in which ornately painted reef fish avoid being eaten. When identifying fish, note that guides may provide different common names for the same species, or conversely, the same names for different species. If you are confused, compare the scientific names (which may not always agree either).

SNORKELING

Snorkeling—a journey into unique underwater world—is a marvelous experience that can be enjoyed by everyone. At Molokini, clear waters, underwater bluffs and gentle swimming with tame fish please novice and experienced snorkeler alike. SCUBA trips can be arranged for those with experience.

Here are a few pointers that will set your mind at ease as well as protect this fragile environment:

1. *Don't worry about sharks.* Hawaii's inshore waters are essentially free of danger-ous sharks during the daytime. Dusk or night snorkeling is not recommended as tiger sharks occasionally swim close to shore after dark. Small sharks (white-tipped or black-tipped) may be seen; they are harmless.
2. *Don't poke your fingers or body into holes or caves.* Hawaii has several species of moray eels and lobsters. Leave cave exploration to those with experience.
3. *Don't touch sea urchins,* especially the black ones with long, skinny spines. Their stings are painful.
4. *Don't walk or rest your feet on the coral reef or on rocks covered with marine life.* All marine invertebrate animals are fragile and easily crushed.
5. *Don't venture into surge channels or narrow crevices when the sea is rough.* The sea is powerful, and even smallish waves can bash your body uncontrollably against rocks, causing scrapes and grazed skin. Coral cuts are superficial yet painful.
6. *Keep the ocean bottom in view.* Remember that Molokini is a tiny volcanic island amidst a deep channel.
7. *Make sure your mask fits perfectly.* Check for leaks around the rubber seal, espe-cially around your temples. Don't be afraid to ask for another.

Jim Maragos

A ubiquitous and common fish is the convict tang or **MANINI** (*Acanthurus sandvicensis*), pictured above. Ancient Hawaiians sometimes cooked the fish with its intestines intact, so that the partly digested *limu* (seaweed) in the stomach could be enjoyed as an accompanying sauce.

Ed Robinson

Ed Robinson

(*top*) This marine "condominium," a large colony of **ELKHORN CORAL** (*Pocillopora eydouxi*) supports varied "tenants": fish, crabs, worms, encrusting algae, sponges, etc. Just as in a real condo, each occupant owns and defends his individual space, yet the area surrounding the living complex is common ground. (*bottom*) **FLAT-TAILED NEEDLEFISH** or *aha* (*Belone platyura*), brilliantly silvery, live close to the water's surface but are harmless to snorkelers.

47

For natural history aficionados, the opportunity to spot tropical seabirds skimming across the water is equally as exciting as seeing a hula girl. A trip to Molokini is such an opportunity, although the density of ocean birds inhabiting Hawaii's major channels is low.

Prior to human contact, all of Hawaii's islands, large and small, supported huge colonies of seabirds. The ancient Hawaiians ate their flesh and utilized the feathers of certain species for feather capes and ornamental *kahili* (royal standards). Today, due to disturbance and predation by introduced mammals, including man, seabirds only breed successfully in wildlife sanctuaries.

A final word concerning "seagulls"—Hawaii has none except rarities. This may seem surprising, especially to residents of mainland coastal areas. Gulls, of which there are many species, inhabit only the temperate zones; warm seas lack sufficient food to support them. Note Maui's paucity of seaweeds and rich intertidal life, important food sources for gulls.

A downy Bulwer's Petrel (*Bulweria bulweri*) chick.

A wildlife biologist holds an adult **BULWER'S PETREL** at Molokini. Rarely seen, this robin-sized seabird flies into the islet late at night, remains a few hours to tend its chick or relieve its mate on the egg, then, with erratic, bat-like flight, whisks out to sea well before dawn. One cannot help but marvel at the instinctive skills enabling these small birds to survive within the perilous environment of the open ocean.

David Boynton

A dark brown inshore seabird, about one foot long, and having slender wings and snowy crown, flies by your boat. It suddenly flutters, then plunges rapidly into the water. Such birds are *terns*, relatives of gulls, either **BROWN NODDIES** (*Anous stolidus*) as shown, or black noddies (*Anous minutus*). The ancient Hawaiians, who called noddies *noio*, were conversant with their habits of associating with small craft. The following is a chant about catching *aku* (skipjack tuna) near Molokini:

> *Hanging there at the gable end*
> *Being watched by a* noio,
>
> *The current is flowing towards Makena*
> *Where swims the* aku.

49

(*below*) A seventeen-inch-long **WEDGE-TAILED SHEARWATER** (*Puffinus pacificus*) reposes at the mouth of its nesting burrow on Molokini. At left is a fluffy chick. Few people see them, but an estimated 1,500 pairs nest here annually from March to November. This type of seabird is called a "shearwater" because its pointed wings dip so close to the water's surface as the bird flies, they seem to "cut" it. Though at dawn and dusk hundreds of wedge-tails hover over Molokini and skim its surrounding waters, by the time snorkeling tours arrive they are all cruising out at sea or tending their eggs deep within earthen burrows. Sunset cruises often turn up seabirds, especially during summer.

Cameron Kepler

Cameron Kepler

Cameron Kepler

(*bottom*) Possibly the most abundant seabird on earth (though this is not evident from a visit to Maui), the sleek, black-and-white **SOOTY TERN** (*Sterna fuscata*) is sometimes seen en route to Molokini. The Hawaiians, who named it *ewaewa*, admired its grace but nevertheless also enjoyed it hot and steaming, fresh from an *imu* (underground oven). The following descriptive chant was composed in 1883 for King Kalakaua's coronation:

> Birds (terns) circle about the sky, poise
> In dipping flight over the waves.

You may be lucky to see other juvenile seabirds such as a **RED-FOOTED BOOBY** or *a* (*Sula sula*), common throughout the Pacific (*top*). Their immatures are mostly brown, whereas the adults are mostly white. **GREAT FRIGATEBIRDS** or *iwa* (*Fregata minor*) occasionally fly high over South Maui's beaches. Their "scissortails" are unmistakable (*center*). Their Hawaiian name means "thief," on account of their habit of stealing fish from other birds, a deft mid-air maneuver.

51

(*above*) Molokini has even more surprises. After its introduced rabbits all perished, several native plants resprang into existence. This succulent, **MOLOKINI IHI** (*Portulaca molokiniensis*) was discovered in 1980. Adapted to dry, rocky and salty locations, Molokini's namesake is one of the rarest species in the world, totalling less than twenty wild plants. Its entire geographic range, Molokini and Kahoolawe, can be seen in this photo of planted individuals at Wailea Point.

(*opposite*) From November to May, Hawaii's official marine mammal, the **HUMP-BACK WHALE** (*Megaptera novaeangliae*) inhabits Maui's waters, including those surrounding Molokini (near cliff in top photo). A characteristic posture is this "fluke-up dive." After inhalation, a one-second gulp which fills the lungs to 100 percent capacity, the whale dives and its tail flukes, 10- to 15-feet broad, rise high into the air.

Whale flukes are like human faces. Their overall shape, patterning, irregularities and scars (from shark bites or barnacles) allow for individual identification. This information is used by the Pacific Whale Foundation, whose researchers are actively involved in whale protection and public education. In addition to calving, a vital aspect of their annual migration from Alaska to Hawaii involves the discarding of ecto-parasitic barnacles. These "hitchhikers" die in Hawaii's warm waters. *As many as one thousand pounds of acorn barnacles have been found attached to a single whale!*

Pacific Whale Foundation

James Hudnall

CHAPTER IV WAILEA

Wailea. In past times the name meant "water belonging to Lea," the goddess of canoe-making. Here, in small villages, people lived in harmonious intimacy with the life-giving sun and bountiful sea, the primary domains of ancient gods and goddesses. Today, Wailea's beauty and activities still revolve around the sun and sea, whose colors comprise her logo (**right**). We assume that the old

Polynesian gods and goddesses are extinct, but were they not different manifestations of universal energy...timeless, powerful, incomprehensible?

At least three million years of evolution were needed to clothe Wailea in her original guise, a primordial raiment which has been basically forgotten. It is generally assumed that before Wailea's present development into a tropical oasis, it was a parched, unproductive wasteland, of little use to anyone. Not so. Wailea's original beauty was never recorded, but telltale fragments from the past—palaeobiology, archaeology and history, together with current biology, geography and geology, enable us to reconstruct a fairly accurate picture. In order to fully appreciate today's Wailea, we begin seven centuries ago.

The first Polynesians to settle on Maui did so along the Wailea-Makena-Kahikinui-Hana coast. The area was so appealing they named it *Kahikinui*, or "big Tahiti," a tribute to their beautiful homeland. This lengthy coastline was the most highly populated region of Maui for at least five centuries. People worked the land for taro and sweet potatoes, and cultivated *kukui* trees and other useful plants.

Unlike Lahaina and Kaanapali, Wailea was not a seat of royalty, smitten with bloody battles and power struggles. Here, Hawaiians lived simple lives—gardening, fishing, eating, playing with children, bartering salt and other commodities with upland families. They welcomed the white man's ways but, in doing so, soon lost their lifestyles, values and spiritual beliefs.

Wailea's village inhabitants (from 1350 A.D.) depended heavily on the sea for their survival. Offshore waters, rocky points, sandy coves, and coral reefs all provided a prolific, and seemingly never-ending supply of fish (*ia*), sea urchins (*wana*), crabs (*papai*), shellfish (*pupu*), and seaweeds (*limu*). Turtles laid copious numbers of eggs in the golden sand. Monk seals hauled out and pupped on the beaches too. Dolphins and humpbacks cavorted in nearshore waters. Contemporary sightings of any of these larger denizens of the sea are always special.

Drinking water was fresh from the numerous streams which furrowed Haleakala's high slopes. Today, an airplane flight over Haleakala's south slope (*p. 57*) or a glance at a relief map of Maui reveals these old gullies, now parched or reduced to intermittent trickles. Hundreds more water-carved gulches sculpture the slopes east of Wailea; some exceed 100 feet deep. Springs also popped up here and there along the coast. A spring which emerged until relatively recently on Polo Beach was undoubtedly a major reason why the original Wailea Point village was established.

Grand Hyatt Hotel

A POLYNESIAN FISHERMAN, poised to strike, awaits his prey in a Grand Hyatt "lagoon." Artist Herb Kane.

Recent analysis of remnant native vegetation indicates that a variety of ecosystems once clothed Haleakala's south slope. The Wailea region supported dry shrublands and forests: *naio* (*Myoporum sandwicense*) and *aalii* (*Dodonaea* species) were abundant.

During these past times too, vast colonies of seabirds—petrels, shearwaters, albatrosses, terns—nested on Hawaii's main islands. Scores of now-extinct, flightless land birds provided easy meals for early Hawaiians: stocky geese (*below*), ibises, and coot-like rails. Migrating shorebirds dotted the shores and hills. *Nene* geese undertook annual travels to the lowlands while molting, where the Hawaiians were adept at chasing and pelting them with stones. Bones from middens, subfossil skeleta in lava tube caves, and early writings on Hawaiian lore speak eloquently, silently, of all these happenings.

Over the past 200 years great changes have taken place. Upslope, *koa* (*Acacia koa*) forests were almost entirely replaced by cattle, goats and forage grasses. Immense fires ravaged the mountainsides. Introduced *kiawe*, cacti, lantana, and other weedy plants filled the void, converting thousands of acres into the spiny wastelands that most people believe have been there since time began. Streams stopped flowing, springs withered. Rainfall decreased drastically, the sun's heat intensified. It became in part a desert, in part marginal ranchlands. Fresh lava flows added more barrenness to the terrain. Avid hunters killed shorebirds mercilessly. Seabirds, turtles, dolphins and seals departed to meet their fates elsewhere. People relocated. We wonder how, and why, anyone lived there.

Wailea is now a tropical oasis studded with multicolored jewels: sparkling golden beaches, turquoise pools, emerald lawns, and immaculately

Douglas Pratt

FLIGHTLESS GEESE of several species have been unearthed from lava tubes and caves not far from Wailea and Makena. They survived well into the Hawaiian era. One is appropriately named *Ptaiochen pau*, a curious combination of Greek and Hawaiian roots meaning "the extinct goose which had a propensity for stumbling into caves." Artistic rendering by Douglas Pratt.

manicured gardens alive with vibrant color. The fact that Wailea (population 1,500) is one of Hawaii's most prestigious master-planned resorts and a winner of landscaping, design, culinary and sporting awards, is evident the moment you enter its boundaries. A creation of Wailea Development Company (a subsidiary of Alexander and Baldwin Company), it covers 1,500 acres, including almost two miles of beaches and lava points. Begun in 1971 and still actively growing, it houses homesites, condominiums, and four luxury hotels (Stouffer Wailea Beach Resort, Maui Inter-Continental Wailea, the Four Seasons, Grand Hyatt), with a fifth, Kea Lani, opening soon.

Wailea abounds with extravagant luxuries aimed at pampering the visitor: lei greetings at the hotels, free movies and cultural events at the shopping village, gourmet dining, Hawaiian crafts (lei-making, hula lessons, quilting, etc.), babysitting and children's programs, sunset cruises, translating and secretarial services, video rooms, chocolates on pillows, etc. For sports enthusiasts, activities include snorkeling, surfing, deep sea fishing, SCUBA diving, golf, tennis, bicycling and fitness programs. At the end of a day, sauna rooms, spas and trained masseurs can relax overworked muscles.

Wailea...an area originally dedicated to Lea, the goddess of canoe-making. Today it is dedicated to a different deity—Pleasure. Lea has been relegated to the dusty annals of Hawaiian history. Even her bird namesake, the wren-like *elepaio*, has deserted Maui. Lea's old wooden outriggers, once crafted with spiritual reverence, still rest safely (albeit in their invisible forms) within the ancient sheds which dot the lonely coast beyond Makena. Although Wailea's old canoes have been superceded by jazzy racers, sailboats, hobie cats, catamarans, and windsurfing rigs, they live on in different forms: the pleasing sight of muscled Hawaiians practicing for the next canoe regatta and a mermaid-guarded, flower-filled replica which graces the Grand Hyatt foyer.

HALEAKALA'S SOUTH SLOPE, today a mixture of goat-eroded deserts and marginal ranchlands, was once clothed with thick forests. Former drainage patterns are chiselled clearly into this vast area.

Wailea Destination Assn.

(*top*) Many **ARCHAEOLOGICAL SITES** have recently been unearthed in the Wailea-Makena area. The most important ones have been placed on both the Hawaii and National Registers of Historic Places. Pictured is a reconstructed, walled enclosure at Wailea Point, from which over 600 artifacts were unearthed. Half were prehistoric items, dating back to 1350 A.D., including fish bones, fishing gear, coral abraders, poi pounders and adzes. This site's original function was as a "boarding house" assisting travelers and fishermen. Its freshwater spring dried up only recently.

(*center*) Replicas of traditional bone fishing hooks.

(*left*) Rare plants thrive along Wailea Point's coastal trail.

The heavens above Wailea light up on a January night as crimson skies blaze with dark clouds and white-hot incandescence.

Randy Hufford/Maui Inter-Continental

(*left*) Historic Wailea about 1987. (*right*) A tiny pocket of fresh water in lava at Cape Kinau is indicative of the many springs which surfaced along the Wailea-Makena-Kahikinui coast. This one harbors minuscule native red shrimps or *opae* (*Halocaradina rubra*).

ART

Wailea is new and international, yet it reflects a unique location and special Hawaiian "roots." The multidimensional art styles of each resort, indoors and out, not only exhibit the general excellence of art on Maui, but have also evolved in new directions. Staggering amounts of money are spent on both permanent "art museums" and periodic art shows. For example, the Maui Inter-Continental hosts an annual Maui Marine Art Expo, a major cultural event in which painters, sculptors and photographers exhibit a multimedia celebration of the marine environment's beauty and fragility. The Grand Hyatt's $30 million art collection, displaying both local and international artists, includes strikingly innovative interpretations of Hawaiian themes. In addition to their permanent "art museums," all resorts offer craft classes and host periodic art shows.

Robert Lyn Nelson

(*below*) "Molokini First Breath," painted in acrylics and oil by Mauian Robert Lyn Nelson, illustrates the characteristic "two-world marine imagery" for which he has become internationally renowned. All colors, patterns and shapes, down to the finest details on the reef fish, are true to life. Each winter, within the royal blue depths off Wailea, baby whales inhale their first gasps of air, although few people are privileged to witness such special events.

Grand Hyatt Resort

KING KAMEHAMEHA THE GREAT, the most renowned chief in Hawaiian history, guards the entrance to the Grand Hyatt. He is clad in ceremonial dress, including a bronzed "feather cape." Prior to Kamehameha's birth (ca. 1755), a prophecy declared that he would become a "killer of chiefs and ruler of all the islands." The ruler at that time, Alapai, insisted that the baby be killed at birth so his mother fled to the Kohala Mountains (Island of Hawaii) for safety. She named him "the lonely one" commemorating his childhood seclusion, but fate triumphed and the feared prophecy came true. Kamehameha united all the islands through vigorous bloody battles, but he was also wise and loving. His favorite wife was Kaahumanu, whose name is memorialized in Kahului's main thoroughfare.

(**top, center**) Two trios of Hawaiian **DANCERS** whirl above carpets of flowers and greenery, Grand Hyatt, while a modern trio adorns the Four Seasons' central gardens (**bottom left**). Amid Stouffer's spacious gardens, **DEMIGOD MAUI** "fishes" up the island of Maui from a stretch of lawn (**bottom right**). Maui, the island's namesake, was a popular and well-loved character in Pacific mythology. His supernatural powers enabled him to perform superhuman feats such as hauling up Hawaii and New Zealand from the bottomless deep, slowing the sun (so his mother's *tapa* could dry better), and reestablishing the fire-making skill on earth after the gods had banished it.

Grand Hyatt Resort

David Franzen/The Four Seasons

The Village Gallery, Lahaina

Frequent art shows display Hawaii's best artists. A tin-roofed green home by Stephen Burr stirs nostalgia in old-timers (**top**), while Richard Pettit's rendering of Hawaii's state fish, the *humuhumunukunukuapuaa* ("the triggerfish with a snout like a pig") invites one to don a mask and snorkel.

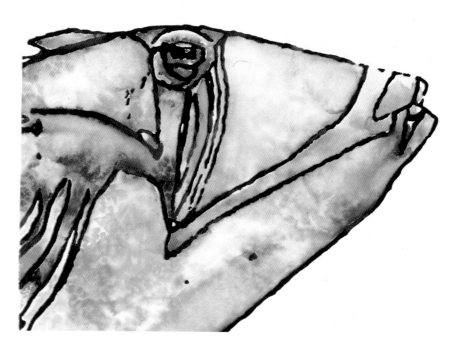

Coast Gallery

A centuries-old Polynesian tradition, the art of **LEI-MAKING** is vibrantly alive on Maui. Flower garlands honor any occasion—an arrival, departure, birthday, graduation, civic speech, concert, job well done, or simply "I love you." Most hotels greet guests with a fresh flower lei , instruction in various techniques is available, and each spring the Maui Inter-Continental Hotel hosts an island-wide lei contest. Fresh flower leis, like Hawaiian music, defy description...enjoy their color, design, scent, and the special glow that derives from wearing them. The photos below illustrate special styles of lei-making. (**left**) "Beaks" of the pale green jade vine intertwine in a definite pattern beside purple vanda orchids threaded in Mauna-loa style. (**right, opposite left**) In *haku*-style leis, flowers are looped and sewn onto a fabric or banana leaf backing.

David Franzen/The Four Seasons

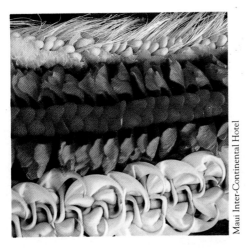

Maui Inter-Continental Hotel

Maui Inter-Continental Hotel

Wailea Destination Association

Maui Inter-Continental Hotel

(*above*) Bedecked with plumeria leis and coronas, little girls wait their turn on stage. (*left*) A corona lei features rosebuds, baby's breath & ferns.

65

Flowers are lavish and abundant at Wailea, indoors and out. Most arrangements utilize Hawaiian-grown greenery and blossoms: orchids, proteas, heliconias, gingers, and anthuriums. (**top left**) Red ginger, *ti* leaves, white orchids, palm leaves and two species of heliconias. (*center*) A spray of Phalaenopsis "White with Red Lips" arches from a mini-garden of ferns. (*bottom left*) 'Sexy pink' heliconia, papyrus and *ti* leaves. (**bottom right**) King proteas, scarlet banksias, 'Sunburst' and 'Rocket' pincushions.

(*left*) Pink gingers, lilies and anthuriums, *obake* anthuriums, *lauae* fern and yellow caribaea heliconia. (*right*) Yellow oncidium orchids, day lilies, and white anthuriums.

(*left*) An artful twig embellishment in an ornamental bromeliad. (*right*) Red anthuriums, red Christmas heliconia, and foliage from 'Indian Summer' banksia.

(*top*) The Grand Hyatt specializes in large, life-size sculptures and intricately detailed murals depicting Hawaiian mythology. In fiery tongues of color and art deco style, artists Robert Evans and Charles Brown portray the VOLCANIC CREATION of Hawaii. (*bottom*) Stouffer's has just undergone extensive recent renovations, which included a complete change of their art decor. Pictured is a beautiful HAWAIIAN QUILT with traditional design. Early missionaries taught Hawaiian women quilting techniques, in which they quickly excelled.

Miscellaneous creative pursuits at Wailea include wood-carving (**top left and right**), on-
site painting (**center**), and tapa (bark-cloth)
designs (**bottom**). Note the *konane* in the bottom photo, an ancient Hawaiian "checkers"
game which uses smooth volcanic stones and
coral chunks for pieces.

WAILEA BEACHES

Sun and sand: prime attractions of Maui. Wailea's superb crescentic beaches, separated by rocky lava points, afford excellent swimming, snorkeling, and bodysurfing, plus unparalleled panoramas of Kahoolawe, Molokini and Lanai. From these vantage points, the West Maui Mountains and Puu Olai also appear on the horizon as domed "islands."

Wailea's golden strands slope gently underwater, bearing minimal coral debris and submerged rocks. From north to south (***bottom to top in photo below***) the beaches are: Keawakapu (see Kihei), Mokapu, Ulua, Wailea and Polo. (Note to aid memories: the first four beaches are in alphabetical order). All have paved, landscaped pathways, clean public facilities and public access roads clearly marked along Wailea Alanui Drive, the main thoroughfare through Wailea. Given today's tranquility, it takes effort to imagine that during the 1940s all Maui's "Gold Coast" beaches were fortified to duplicate enemy beachheads. More than 4,000 men underwent rigorous training in activities such as reconnaissance and demolition. Remnants of concrete bunkers can still be found on a few rocky points. Back then the beaches barely saw footprints.

Wailea Destination Association

(***opposite***) Two views of **MOKAPU BEACH,** a lovely stretch of sand fronting Stouffer's. *Mokapu,* an abbreviation of *moku kapu,* means "sacred island," and refers to a former rocky offshore islet which was obliterated during World War II demolition exercises.

Beautiful **ULUA BEACH** between Stouffer's and the Inter-Continental, is one of Maui's prime snorkeling locations, especially the rocky section at its north end (*on right of top photo*). Top photo looks west towards distant Kahoolawe, while bottom photo is oriented south. The beach is named after *ulua*, a general term for jackfish (Family Carangidae), whose many species inhabit Hawaii's waters. *Ulua* are voracious carnivores that feed on fish and shrimps, generally live in schools, and are eagerly hunted for their scrumptious flesh.

Wailea Destination Association

The widest and longest of all, WAILEA BEACH, backed by the Four Seasons and Grand Hyatt Resorts, arches from the Inter-Continental Hotel to Wailea Point. At its south end is a curved wooden bridge which begins a half-mile scenic trail around a rocky lava point landscaped with native coastal plants, and which leads to the next alluring strand, Polo Beach. Wailea Beach is also pictured on the following pages.

Gold, blue and white. Glorious **POLO BEACH** and its frothy shorebreak are crowned by the gentle dome of distant Kahoolawe (*top*). This strand was considered part of Wailea Beach by old-timers, therefore was never given an Hawaiian name. However, during the cattle-ranching days earlier this century, it was called Dead Horse Beach. Horses and cattle sauntered down the mountain from Ulupalakua Ranch to drink from the natural spring that emerged from the sand near the rocks (now below the present walkway). That wasn't a flattering name for such a lovely beach, so a new name was given to it when Wailea's construction began, "Ke One o Polo" ("the sands of Polo").

(*top*) Polo Beach, south of Wailea Point and fronting the Polo Beach Club and new Kea Lani Resort, offers good snorkeling near the rocks. (*bottom*) To its south lies cozy Palauea Beach.

BEACH PLANTS

Wailea's original shrublands and coastal herblands were first replaced by *kiawe* and introduced grasses, and later by manicured gardens. Skirting the picturesque peninsula called Wailea Point is a beautifully maintained, half-mile **COASTAL TRAIL**. A particularly notable feature is its superb landscaping which comprises approximately fifty native coastal plant species, fifteen percent of which are extremely rare. This public pathway is also an excellent location from which to whale-watch or enjoy the foaming waters gushing through narrow clefts and crashing against crinkly lava. What an enigma that an exclusive, multimillion-dollar housing project has an ocean frontage that resembles Hawaii's original coastline more closely than any other location in Hawaii, including coastal preserves! Some of the world's rarest plants are here; several species (for example, false jade plant) are represented by more individuals than biologists have ever seen in the wild. The 10,000-odd native plants along this trail are a tribute to the conservation awareness of its developer, Clyde "Bud" Wagner, the expertise of Maluhia Farms native plant landscaping company, and the efforts of others who, in diverse ways, have contributed to the welfare of Hawaii's dwindling native flora. (***below***) **HAWAIIAN COTTON** or *mao* (*Gossypium sandwicense*), native to South Maui but extremely rare in the wild, has recently contributed to the genetic improvement of agricultural cotton. American breeders use *mao* to produce a hardy strain of cotton that is very resistant to insect pests such as aphids. This native hibiscus, found nowhere else in the world, has less "fluff" than regular cotton, but has the potential to enormously reduce pesticide use, saving farmers large amounts of money and reducing environmental pollution.

(top) TREE HELIOTROPES (*Tournefortia argentea*) are often encountered along "Gold Coast" beaches, as they can tolerate sun, salt, sandy soils and a relative lack of fresh water. Their tiny white flowers, arranged in tight spiral clusters, are reminiscent of their cousins, forget-me-nots. The masses of little green fruits, snuggling together like floral octopi, can germinate even in hot sand.

(center) A prostrate relative of tree heliotrope, **HINAHINA-KA-KAHAKAI** (*Heliotropum anomalum*) was so special to the old Hawaiians they designated it the island flower of Kahoolawe. Formerly widespread around all coastlines, this creeper now occurs in only a few protected spots. Its Hawaiian name means "silvery plant by the ocean." It is no longer used for celebrations that call for leis made from official "island flowers" as it is quite rare now; "old man's beard" is its substitute.

(below) This beautiful **YELLOW HIBISCUS** with a maroon center (*Hibiscus calyphyllus*) is the only large "native" hibiscus at Wailea Point. Formerly thought to be a rare Kauai species, botanists now consider it a naturalized ornamental from Africa.

(*top*) Abundant on beaches from Kihei to Makena, natural or planted, is the sprawling succulent shrub, **BEACH NAUPAKA** (*Scaevola sericea*). Ancient Hawaiians, who called it *naupaka-kahakai*, meaning "naupaka-by-the-edge-of-the-sea," were puzzled by its unusual "half-flowers." In attempting to unravel this quirk of Nature, they told several touching tales, one version of which follows:

Many years ago, two lovers strolled along a beach, hand in hand. Soon their romance turned to anger and Puna, the girl, snatched a naupaka-kahakai blossom (which legend relates was a whole flower in those days), and ripped it in half. She refused to speak to her boyfriend again until he brought her a new, complete blossom. As soon as she had torn the flower, the gods changed all Hawaii's naupaka flowers into "half-flowers," the mountain as well as the seashore species. Puna's lover searched in vain for an entire blossom and eventually died of a broken heart, leaving Puna to regret her outrage. The flowers, many generations later, still grow incompletely.

(P.S. The biological reason for the *naupaka*'s "half-flower" is simple: the five-petalled blossom has a deep slit between two petals, allowing insects easier access to its pollen.) The marble-like berries are called *huahekili*—"hailstones" (*center*).

(*bottom right*) Only a handful of **FALSE JADE PLANTS** (*Scaevola coriacea*) are left in the wild. (*bottom left*) **ILIMA** (*Sida fallax*), Oahu's island flower, still makes very special leis, requiring around 500 blossoms per lei.

(***top left***) **PUAKALA** (*Argemone glauca*), a native white-flowering poppy, was an important medicinal plant in old Hawaii, used primarily as a painkiller for toothaches. (***top right***) **NAIO** (*Myoporum sandwicense*) was formerly a major component of Wailea's coastal shrublands. Last century, when sandalwood supplies became depleted, *naio*, a "false sandalwood" was substituted. Some wild trees still grow in Kanaio (beyond Makena). (***center***) **OHAI** (*Sesbania tomentosa*), a very rare native legume. (***bottom left***) For most plants, sand is a highly unstable substrate, weak in nutriment and too salty to sustain life. However, the **SEASIDE MORNING GLORY** or *pohuehue* (*Ipomoea brasiliensis*) thrives on hot beaches, stabilizing dunes with its sturdy vines. In ancient times it was used in a ritual for inducing the surf to rise. Hopeful surfers thrashed its stems on the water, simultaneously chanting to the gods. Its gay, mauve, funnel-shaped blossoms are surprisingly fragile. Pick one and it wilts almost immediately. Note the butterfly-like leaves.

CULTURE AND ENTERTAINMENT

Entertainment at Wailea—indeed at all Maui's luxury resorts—offers the best of island talent as well as periodic mainland groups. Naturally, Hawaiian music and dance are priorities. Periodic festivals are highlighted by costumes representing Hawaiian royalty or *alii*, ancient hula dancers (***opposite***), and traditional dress from other Pacific islands. Very special are the **WAIEHU SONS** (***below***), one of the state's major entertainment groups, who have delighted listeners at Stouffer since 1978. Born in Waiehu (Maui) of Polynesian heritage, they are truly "sons of Maui." They compose, sing and play Hawaiian music using an instrumental accompaniment of slack-key guitar, *ukulele* and string bass. Of interest here is the origin of the *ukulele*, indispensable to Hawaiian music for decades but originally brought to Hawaii in 1879 by Portuguese immigrants. The name *ukelele* means "leaping flea," nickname of Edward Purvis, a small quick man who popularized this instrument.

(*opposite*) **ANCIENT HULA DANCERS** are adorned with traditional *palapalai* ferns (*Microlepia strigosa*) and skirts dating from the 19th century. The gourd rattles or *uliuli* are used for drumming as well as in the dance movements.

Wailea Destination Association

Hula. Along with its allies—coconut palms, hibiscus flowers, and sunny beaches—hula dancing epitomizes Hawaii. Although we associate this gentle dance with women, its most ancient form was the exclusive domain of men (*kane*). Life in former times was very spiritual: music, poetry and the hula, for example, were inseparable from religion and recreation. This was primarily due to the absence of a written language until the 19th century.

The Hawaiians were, and still are, very musical, thus their tales, sorrows, genealogies, prayers and joyful expressions were all expressed in poetic, rhythmic chants: today's *kahiko* or "ancient hula." These chants, greatly cherished, were passed down in meticulous detail from one generation to another. When the strict missionaries arrived in Hawaii (1820s) they were shocked beyond belief by hula dancing, and assiduously set about to abolish it. However, King Kalakaua ("The Merrie Monarch") began reviving it in the 1880s by sponsoring nightly performances of a *hula halau* (dance troupe) at Iolani Palace in Honolulu. Within the last 20 years, hula has enjoyed an additional rejuvenation and expansion, especially **MEN'S HULA** (*below*).

In past centuries, hulas were customarily danced in joyful gratitude to the gods for their blessings, and audiences shared in the celebration. Since music and dance still transcend time and space, recapture the magic of the hula's essential spirit as you watch the performers.

Wailea Destination Association

Wailea Destination Association

Hawaii is a three-way crossroads of Asia, the Pacific and North America. As such it has benefitted from the traditions of other cultures such as Tahiti (**left**). A muumuu-clad dancer (**right**), wearing **SHELL LEIS** or *lei pupu*, performs an *auwana* (modern hula), where the hand and body movements synchronize with the music. This contrasts with *kahiko* (ancient hula), where the hand and body movements represent an interpretation of the chant, not intended to be melodic. (**below**) Children, wearing twisted *ti*-leaf leis, interpret **KAHIKO HULA**.

Carol Zahorsky/The Four Seasons

All Wailea's resorts specialize in cultural attractions. Specific dates are listed in the telephone book's cultural calendar, beach guides, *Maui Inc.* & *Mauian* magazines, and *The Maui News*. Many concerts and festivities are free at the **WAILEA SHOPPING VILLAGE** (*top*). (*center left*) **SEASHELL WIND INSTRUMENTS** or *pu* are still used throughout the Pacific for special summons. (*center right*) Charlie Dapitan, a *kamaaina* **GUITARIST**. (*bottom*) **JULY 4** is always a time for celebration.

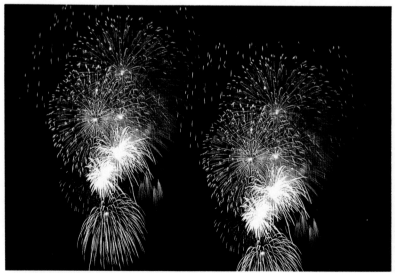

Bob Abraham

Four Seasons

Four Seasons

"ROYAL COURTS" are held on special Hawaiian celebrations such as Lei Day (May 1), Kamehameha Day (June 11), and Aloha Week (fall).

Maui Inter-Continental Hotel

Miscellaneous entertainment includes local stories and songs (*mele*) by much-loved *kamaaina* **AUNTY EMMA SHARP (now deceased)** and Jesse Nakooka (*left*), festivals (*center right*) and **SANTA CLAUS** (*bottom*). (*center left*) Fashion shows include Hawaii-made clothing for the larger figure.

Steve Read

Maui Inter-Continental Hotel

(*right*) One of Maui's most treasured musical highlights is the annual visit of Hawaii's only professional, internationally recognized orchestra, the **HONOLULU SYMPHONY**. Concert programs throughout the state embrace a wide variety of musical tastes: a full classical repertoire from Bach to the 20th century, light classical, ballet, opera, Hawaiian/ethnic music, jazz, Broadway, humorous and romantic music. Special artists include local entertainers, youth competition winners, internationally noted soloists and gifted island singers. Pictured is part of the symphony's wind section (*left to right*): Norman Foster, James Moffitt, Paul Barrett, Marsha Schweitzer, William Oldfather.

Kyle Rothenborg/Honolulu Symphony

Bob Abraham/Maui Symphony

The **MAUI SYMPHONY ORCHESTRA**, begun in 1979 and composed of both professional and amateur musicians, is a non-profit, volunteer organization playing classical and light music. Its members include physicians, businessmen, students, a model, retired federal employees, and teachers. The symphony plays several times annually at Wailea.

D I N I N G

    Wailea's delectable and varied cuisine, internationally renowned, includes Hawaiian, Oriental (especially Japanese), American, French, Italian, and seafood. A bounty of freshly prepared edibles is available from dawn till midnight from poolside cafs, coffee shops, pizza parlors, "happy hour" bars, gourmet and ethnic restaurants, and lavish Sunday brunches. Eat in a bathing suit, a muumuu, a spangled gown, or a nightie (room service only!). Wailea features several of Maui's most prestigious **RESTAURANTS**. Winners of the acclaimed Travel Holiday award include La Perouse (Inter-Continental, *center, left*) and Raffles (Stouffer). (*bottom Left*) "Maui Captures the Sun," an art piece by Shige Yamada, presides over the Grand Hyatt's Grand Dining Room (*bottom right*). Cafes, generally located near pools or beaches, are very casual, such as the Cabana Cafe at the Four Seasons. (*center right*) Gentle strains of Hawaiian music from the Waiehu Sons aid digestion at Stouffers.

Maui Inter-Continental Hotel

Stouffer Wailea Beach Resort

Grand Hyatt Resort

David Franzen/The Four Seasons

Luau, the scrumptious banquets offered by many hotels in the islands, are bountiful arrays of staple foods and delicacies gathered from centuries of intermingling peoples: ancient Polynesians, Chinese, Japanese, Filipinos, Americans and the multiethnic residents of contemporary Hawaii. Foods represented by Polynesian Hawaii are *poi* (pounded taro), sweet potatoes, *haupia* (coconut pudding), and *kalua* pig. The latter is a whole pig cooked slowly in an underground oven (*imu*) by a process combining baking and steaming. Here Hawaiian men, attired in lava-lavas with tapa designs and *kukui* nut leis, extract a ready-to-eat **KALUA PIG** from an *imu.* The pork, deliciously succulent and subtly smoky, is deboned, sliced and shredded in the traditional manner. Desserts (forget your waistline) may include guava mousse, and *mai tai* cream pie. Luau entertainment typically focuses on Polynesian dancing and intensely rhythmical music. The dancers' scintillating energy and richly colored costumes transport us temporarily to the unique cultures of their far-flung, native isles.

Maui Inter-Continental Hotel

Maui Inter-Continental Hotel

MAI TAI CREAM PIE

"GOLD COAST" FLOWERS AND LANDSCAPING

Hawaii's native plants, having evolved in isolation for millions of years, are strikingly different from familiar ones in temperate areas. Fully 90 percent of Hawaii's native plants are found nowhere else in the world. Hundreds of tropical plants, mostly from other countries, form the bulk of island landscaping. It is these ornamentals which enhance the natural beauty of the Kihei-Wailea-Makena area.

(*top, center*) Simple but beguiling, **PLUMERIAS** (*Plumeria* spp.) evoke unique island sentiments. Abundant everywhere below 3,000 feet elevation, their enchanting fragrance bespeaks the romance of full moons shining through coconut palms, tropical luxuriance, and sunny weather. They are especially appealing when fashioned into leis or worn in the hair. Remember girls—the flower behind your right ear means you are "available;" behind your left, you are "taken."

(*bottom*) **LAUAE FERN** (*Phymatosorus scolopendria*) is a shapely two-foot-high ground cover. Pronounced *la-wah-ee*, this lowly member of the plant kingdom is easily identified by its finger-like frond divisions and large round spore-cases.

(***top***) The naturally braided stems of
THUNBERGIA VINES (*Thunbergia fragrans*) dangle over balconies. (***center***)
IXORA (*Ixora* spp.) flowers are common
as hedges, shrubs or in low massed
plantings (even at fast food restaurants).
Their spherical masses of scarlet "stars" are
composed of dozens of individual, long-
tubular flowers. The unusual name is
derived from the Hindu god Iswara, to
whom ixora flowers were offered in their
Asian homelands. (***bottom left***) The
SPIDER LILY (*Pancratium littorale*) is a
fragrant ornamental from tropical
America. Note the delicate beauty of its
central tissues, an inspiration for the
flower's original name *Hymenocallis*, the
"heavenly hymen!" (***bottom right***)
BOUGAINVILLEA (*Bougainvillea spectabilis*) is a perennial bloomer from
Brazil. Its full sprays of dazzling brilliance,
occurring in a kaleidoscope of colors, are
due to *colored leaves* rather than *petals*.
Remember that its viney branches are
copiously endowed with sharp spines which
litter the ground beneath. *Always wear footwear and tread carefully around it.*

(*top*) A native of the western Pacific, **RED GINGER** (*Alpinia purpurata*) is a particular favorite around hotel entrances and beside running streams. Its baby plants develop right within the colorful flowerhead. (*center*) The **RED HIBISCUS** (*Hibiscus* spp.), Hawaii's official state flower, is similarly ubiquitous. Single blossoms last one or two days with or without water. Pick some for decorations—more will appear on the bush the next morning as if by magic. Dried red hibiscus flowers, used in some herbal teas, blend well with aromatic herbs such as mint and lemon grass. (*bottom right*) Brilliant yellow, orange, pink, bronze, red and green leaves typify **CROTONS** (*Codiaeum variegatum*), often planted in hedges. The original Pacific island species bore basically green leaves but horticulturalists have "improved on Nature," producing an array of bright-hued tropical novelties. (*bottom left*) Yellow-flowered **HAU** (*Hibiscus filiaceus*), introduced over 1000 years ago by Polynesian settlers, is common around waterslides and pathways.

(*top*) **PINK OLEANDER** (*Nerium oleander*) adds gaiety to roadsides, hotel entryways and parking lots. Never use oleander's stems for roasting hot dogs as its sap is poisonous.

(*center*) The **SLIPPER FLOWER** (*Pedilanthes tithymaloides*) native to the West Indies, is adapted to arid conditions like a cactus.

(*bottom right*) **AFRICAN TULIP TREE** (*Spathodea campanulata*) is unrelated to true tulips. Its frilly asymmetrical blossoms emerge from a tight circle of curved buds.

The **MANILA** or "Christmas" Palm (*Veitchia merrillii*), originating in the Philippines, is easily recognized in fall and winter by its scarlet clusters of acorn-like seeds. The seeds are occasionally used for leis.

(***top left***) Showers of delicate little red bells may be spotted everywhere in Kihei and Wailea. They belong to the **CORAL PLANT** (*Russelia equisitiformis*), a native of Mexico related to snapdragons. (***center***) A fragrant beauty from India, **YELLOW GINGER** or *awapuhi-melemele* (*Hedychium flavescens*) bears myriad blossoms which may be threaded into delicate leis. (***bottom left***) Huge, leathery, holey leaves characterize **MONSTERA** (*Monstera deliciosa*), a tropical American vine which bears long cylindrical fruits which, when ripe, resemble the taste of pureed pineapples, bananas and soursops. Monstera is related to calla lilies and taro. (***bottom right***) Several species of shower trees enhance Wailea's immaculate gardens and landscaped roads. Their billowy masses of yellow, creams, pinks, reds and bronzy yellows burst into bloom during summer and fall. Pictured is the **RAINBOW SHOWER** (*Cassia* x *nealae*).

(*top left*) The **SAGO PALM** (*Cycas revoluta*), an ornamental from subtropical Japan is commonly cultivated in warm climates and in conservatories. Its starchy pith is so nutritious that this attractive plant was formerly treasured by the Japanese army as an emergency ration. Cycads are not true palms but are "living fossils" dating back 200 million years. (***center left***) **SPRAY OF GOLD** (*Galphimia gracilis*) is originally from Mexico, where its descriptive Spanish name translates to "rain of gold." The small, clustered flowers are starlike. (***bottom***) **PARROT'S BEAK HELICONIA** (*Heliconia psittacorum*), two to three feet high, comes in several charming varieties, all reminiscent of gaudy parrots. A native of tropical America, here it adds gaiety to Stouffer Wailea Beach Resort's entrance. (***top right***) Orchid trees with pink, white, or lavender flowers and butterfly shaped leaves originated in both Asia and Central America, where they were used for food, medicine and tannins. Pictured is the stunning **HONG KONG ORCHID TREE** (*Bauhinia blakeana*).

SPORTS

Sporting activities are extremely popular at Wailea. Wailea's climate is considered "perfect" by some. Sunny days occur year-round, temperatures range from 63°F (March) to 91°F (August, daytime), and rainfall averages about 10 inches per year. Summers generally have no rain.

Championship golf and tennis are Wailea's major sporting attractions. Inland of the beaches they serve as the major focal points for most visitors. The two (almost three) verdant fairways, complete with putting greens, driving ranges, club house and pro shop, are ranked as some of the most beautiful in the nation. The tennis facilities are superb, also taking in the glorious views of 10,000-foot Haleakala, the offshore islands of Kahoolawe, Molokini, and Lanai, Puu Olai (Makena), the West Maui Mountains, the expansive sky and the Pacific Ocean.

In these days of conservation awareness it is imperative that every citizen of the world realizes that water resources are not unlimited. Millions of gallons of water daily are piped into Wailea—especially the golf courses—to keep it green and beautiful. Unfortunately the West Maui aquifer, which contains water accumulated for thousands of years, is becoming depleted at an alarming rate as the "Gold Coast" expands. Geologists estimate that 90% of its waters have now been tapped. Upcountry Maui residents live with frequent, and strict, water shortages from East Maui reservoirs. There is not much visitors or residents can do about this, but please be aware that playing golf and basking in the beauty of Wailea's man-induced oasis is a very special luxury. Do not waste water unnecessarily. If you are politically active, please discourage further development on Maui.

Other year-round sporting activities at Wailea, easier on Maui's limited resources, include snorkeling, bodysurfing, surfing, boogieboarding, sailing, and windsurfing. However, since Wailea lies to the lee of Maui's largest mountain, the trade winds do not always wrap around to create perfect conditions for sports dependent on wind direction and speed.

Wailea Destination Association

Wailea Destination Association

WAILEA'S ORANGE GOLF COURSE features Puu Olai as a stunning backdrop. Designed by Arthur Jack Snyder, this splendid fairway, with its dramatic 180-degree panoramas, was ranked by the American Society of Golf Architects in the top one percent of U.S. courses built since 1962.

Wailea Destination Association

Two velvety championship **GOLF FAIRWAYS**, named Orange and Blue and soon the Gold course to match Wailea's logo, meander through gently undulating *kiawe* forests.

Wailea Destination Association

Surrounded by viridescent fairways, the **WAILEA TENNIS CLUB** is the largest in the state. *World Tennis Magazine* lists it among the top 20 tennis resorts in the nation. Wailea takes pride not only in its professional tournaments and eleven Plexipave courts (three lighted at night), but in its additional three grass courts, which have earned it the nickname "Wimbledon West." Matches on the lawn courts come in the true spirit of Wimbledon—with coffee and, in season, strawberries and cream. Year-round activities include daily instruction by resident pros using the latest technological aids.

Wailea Destination Association

John Severson

Maui Inter-Continental Wailea

The **WAILEA SPEED CROSSING**, a colorful and exciting windsurfing and catamaran regatta, is held every summer at Wailea Beach. Both professionals and amateurs compete in this seven-mile race to Molokini and back. The all-day festivities are heralded by daredevil hanggliders soaring down from high on Haleakala and landing on the beach beside the regatta's sponsor, the Maui Inter-Continental Wailea Hotel.

Opened in 1978, luxurious Stouffer Wailea Beach Resort is a five-star rated hotel with 347 guest rooms, tastefully set amid fifteen beautifully landscaped acres adjoining the second of Wailea's sandy stretches, Mokapu Beach. Its slightly elevated terrain allows for contoured lawns, lush mini-forests and colorful tropical gardens through which streams meander and waterfalls tumble (*opposite, top right*).

Each arriving guest is greeted with a lei (*opposite, top left*) and access to a staggering number of luxuries and world-class services. Stouffer's emanates a gracious, intimate ambience which reflects Hawaiian warm-heartedness. Stouffer's boasts the honor of having received the AAA five-diamond awards for eleven consecutive years. Its room specialties include native *koa* furniture, refrigerator, individual air-conditioning controls, matching "his" and "her" *hapi* coats (Japanese robes), and private *lanai* (porch) facing the beach, gardens, or Haleakala. Outdoor activities include bike tours, outrigger canoeing, catamaran cruises with picnics, reef tours, and instructions in weaving head-leis. Don't miss the gentle music of Maui's Waiehu Sons while you are here.

(*opposite, bottom left*) Vibrant greenery and waterfalls add romantic charm to a **WEDDING CEREMONY** at Stouffer's. "Wedding packages" may include a license, official, wedding cake, photography, rental car, champagne, complimentary fruit bowl, torchbearer, conchshell blower, music, leis, bridal bouquet, silver champagne glass, gown rental, dinner and up to four days in a deluxe, oceanview bridal suite.

Stouffer Wailea Beach Resort

Stouffer's pool is set amid shady greenery beside an outdoor café and spacious lawns.

Maui Inter-Continental Resort

Centered on a picturesque rocky point separating crescentic Ulua and Wailea beaches, the Maui Inter-Continental Resort nestles within 22 acres of spacious lawns and gardens. The first of Wailea's hotels to open (1976), it has undergone extensive renovation but continues to maintain a relaxed "old-fashioned" charm. Its seven low-rise buildings and one seven-story tower are designed to maximize the number of guest rooms with ocean views.

The Maui Inter-Continental, five-star rated with 550 rooms, offers an astounding number of services and specialties. These include a hydro-therapy spa, multilingual concierge/guest relations, hula lessons, video game room, large conference rooms, and clinics for windsurfing, hobie cats and sailboats. They offer "tennis packages," host tennis competitions, lei contests, windsurfing meets, and present outstanding luaus with trans-Pacific entertainment.

All rooms have private lanais with remote cable TV and minibars, while suites have hairdryers, full vanities and refrigerators.

Maui Inter-Continental Resort

(top & lower right) A coastal walkway connecting the two beaches, shady and spacious, is particularly lovely at sunset. *(lower left)* An annual lei contest is sponsored by this resort on Lei Day (see under Art).

Grand Hyatt Wailea Resort and Spa

The Grand Hyatt is indeed grand. Fronting Wailea Beach, between the Maui Inter-Continental and Four Seasons, it is replete with architectural specialties and distinctive gardens, all interconnected by elaborate waterways and fountains. One garden incorporates a Japanese restaurant Kincha ("Golden Tea"). Styled after a country inn and using 800 tons of rock imported from the base of Mount Fuji, Kincha features private *tatami* rooms, a *sushi* bar, authentic art pieces and ancient stone lanterns.

A statue of King Kamehameha presides over the entrance waterfall, which dips into an abyss and reappears in a pool within the flower-filled atrium. Large artworks from Europe, Asia, and Hawaii confer a very international flavor. Nations continue to blend in the 50,000 square-foot Spa Grande: Swiss shower rooms, Japanese *furo*, tropical seaweed wraps and baths, waterfall massages, etc.

Other specialties include a formal seaside wedding chapel, saltwater lagoon with tropical fish, and a children's "wonderland" complete with computer learning center, video game room, and infant care center. Its list of services read like "Everything you've always wanted but were afraid to ask for."

Grand Hyatt Resort

104

Grand Hyatt Resort

Grand Hyatt Resort

Grand Hyatt Resort

Grand Hyatt Resort

(**top left**) Hawaiian petroglyph art; (**top right**) a *limu* (seaweed) bath at the spa; (**center left**) Kincha, the Japanese restaurant/inn, with rocks from Mt. Fuji in the foreground; (**center right**) a hibiscus-decorated swimming pool; and (**bottom**) the open-air atrium with canoes and Hawaiian mermaid.

Grand Hyatt Resort

Four Seasons Resort Wailea

The luxurious Four Seasons Resort *(below)*, opened in 1990, fronts beautiful Wailea Beach between the Grand Hyatt and Wailea Point *(opposite left)*. Its architecture features a distinctive open-air design, replete with pools, fountains, artworks, and abundant orchids and flower arrangements. Almost all of the 380 large guest rooms have ocean views. Luxuries include oversize marble bathrooms, 24-hour room service, hair dryers, terry robes, in-room safes, and maids twice daily.

Amenities and services reflect cosmopolitan refinement. Special touches at the pool are: chilled Evian spray misters to refresh sunbathers, butler-passed iced face towels, and iced water delivery. Additional services include 24-hour multi-lingual concierge, video library, and complimentary valet parking. Attention is paid to every detail, especially in the suites which boast private saunas, telescopes and phones by the commode. Approached by a drive lined with royal palms, the entryway incorporates classical columns which set the mood for the resort's high-ceilinged elegance. Water—pools, ponds, waterfalls, fountains—forms a focal point of the indoor-outdoor decor. Artworks from East, West and Hawaii include lustrous *koa* tables, a vivid mural of early Hawaii and a wooden bowl that has been shaved almost to translucence. A concrete walkway and curved wooden bridge at the south end of the beach begin the quarter-mile native plant coastal trail around Wailea Point, to Polo Beach fronting the Kealani Resort.

David Franzen/The Four Seasons

The Four Seasons

David Franzen/The Four Seasons

Harvey Lloyd/The Four Seasons

David Franzen/The Four Seasons

Wailea Destination Association

CONDOMINIUMS

Since Wailea is a planned resort, its condominiums are clustered in landscaped villages nestled within exquisite gardens and sweeping lawns. These Wailea Villas embody multiple amenities such as swimming pools, putting greens, Jacuzzis, recreational pavilions, paddle tennis courts, shuffleboard, and access to certain hotel activities. The first three condominium villages to be built—Ekahi, Elua and Ekolu ("one," "two," "three" in Hawaiian)—are representative of Wailea's outstanding residential complexes. (*top*) **WAILEA EKAHI** and (*bottom*) **WAILEA ELUA** fronting Ulua Beach *(center photo)*.

WAILEA POINT *(opposite, top)*, a deluxe residential community and award winner of Hawaii's 1986 "Parade of Homes," is situated on a lava peninsula separating two sparkling beaches. No expense was spared in the selection of its top-of-the-line materials from all over the world, making it outstanding in design, construction and finish: *koa* cabinetry, outdoor bricks composed of crushed cinders and coral, corrosion-resistant copper sheathing, and cedar shutters.

Wailea Destination Association

Foster Hull/Wailea Point

(*left*) Wailea Point in 1987. (*right*) A **WESTERLY VIEW** from Wailea Point native plant trail (see Beach Plants) across Polo Beach to distant Kahoolawe. (*below*) Pacific waters gently shower the point's lava mounds, providing a "crab's-eye view" of distant Puu Olai.

CHAPTER V MAKENA

South of Wailea lies Makena (pron. *ma-kenn-ah*), another resort area richly endowed with priceless golden beaches, crystalline waters and expansive views. How appropriate that its Hawaiian name means "abundance!" This, the hottest and driest part of Maui serviced by public roads, emanates a definite sense of solitude quite different from any other coastal area on Maui. Here, one also senses an indefinable primordial ambience, perhaps stemming from its proximity to Maui's freshest lava flow (1790) and its plethora of archaeological sites. Makena's biological and cultural history parallels that of Wailea. The area was originally clothed in lowland dry forests and coastal shrublands. Upslope its forests merged into expanses of the exquisite native hardwood, *koa*. The Southwest Rift, a sharply defined ridgeline studded with cinder cones and extending *mauka* (upslope) from Puu Olai (locally called "Round Hill"), is Makena's most outstanding topographic feature. Historically, this rift played an important role in the distribution of ancient villages along Haleakala's south coast: its steep slopes gave birth to far more streams than the slopes above Wailea and Kihei. Villages were thus more numerous in and beyond Makena than in the areas already discussed. Even though today most forests are gone, Ulupalakua Ranch is the greenest portion of Haleakala's leeward slopes. This is because

Sheila Conant

Several species of dolphins inhabit both deep and shallow waters around the Hawaiian Islands. Lucky people may spot them near the rocky points or from boats traveling to and from Molokini.

Cameron Kepler

An inflatable canoe rests on clear gentle waters, Cape Kinau.

clouds tend to accumulate midway up the ridgeline from Makena to the crater. Fish, birds, seaweeds, and useful plants were all plentiful too.

The first Westerners to set foot on Maui landed at La Perouse Bay in 1786; in doing so they renamed the bay, began mapping, described Maui's native inhabitants for the first time, and initiated changes that continue to the present day. Over the years, the major alterations to Makena have been cattle ranching, the replacement of its pristine vegetation with forage grasses and *kiawe* scrubland, and resort development. Although the climate has always been fairly dry, during the last 200 years water supplies have diminished and the sun has become more intense.

Located at the tail end of Maui's "Gold Coast," Makena has for decades been special to Mauians. Its development has not been without marked local resistance. As early as 1973 the State of Hawaii established the Ahihi-Kinau Natural Area Reserve. Fortunately, Makena's largest expanse of sand and the last accessible swimming, snorkeling and bodysurfing beach for forty-three miles is soon to become a State Park. This famous strand, known variously as Oneloa, Big, Makena, or Hippie Beach, is still a popular spot for overnight camping, but water and facilities are lacking.

Wailea Destination Association

Arms outstretched, an Hawaiian woman symbolizes her lineage from Maui's ancient culture, rooted on Haleakala's south slope from the 12th century.

Cameron Kepler

Cameron Kepler

(*top*) Loose schools of **BLACK TRIGGERFISH** (*Melichthys niger*) snap up microscopic plankton suspended above the reef. (*bottom*) Hawaiian **MONK SEALS**, now rarely seen in Maui's waters, were once abundant on Makena's beaches. Today an endangered species, monk seals are restricted to remote islands and atolls in the Hawaiian Islands National Wildlife Refuge, hundreds of miles northwest of Honolulu.

115

MAKENA BEACHES

Makena's stunning beaches—some of the most beautiful on Maui—are rapidly losing their isolation. Up till the early 1980s locals could drive along the dusty track in jeeps and old pickup trucks, turn to bounce over sandy scrublands, and end up at some gorgeous stretch of pristine sand. Who cared what the beach was called. Grab a can of beer...jump into the waves.

These days beach names are more important if you are selective about your picnic spot. However, they are confusing because of their naming and renaming by geographers, locals, fishermen, hippies, and recent developers. From north to south, Makena's six most-often-used beaches are: (1) Poolenalena (divided by three small rocky points; the central cove is Chang's or Paipu Beach); (2) Makena Bay or Landing, which includes Keawalai; (3) Maluaka or "Maui Prince Beach" (sometimes erroneously called "Makena Beach"); (4) Oneuli (usually incorrectly pronounced as "Onouli") or Black Sand Beach. Located just north of Puu Olai, its southern portion is sometimes known as Naupaka Beach, a name which has been erroneously applied to the entire Oneuli Beach; (5) Puu Olai Beach, also called Little, Little Makena, or "Nude" Beach; and (6) Oneloa, Makena, Big, or "Hippie" Beach (the last name derives from an influx of hippies during the 1960s.)

All are excellent swimming and snorkeling areas, especially favored by bodysurfers and surfers. **(below) POOLENALENA BEACH**. Its name means "yellow head" after a dark, yellow-streaked boulder (visible from the road and nearby golf course), a local landmark.

(*top*) Still undeveloped, Poolenalena Beach Park is one of the last remaining beaches where Maui's native people (*bottom*) and long-time residents can retreat for a quiet picnic.

117

Fronting Makena Surf condo is a portion of Poolenalena beach known as Paipu or **CHANG'S BEACH**.

Maui Prince Hotel

An aerial **SOUTHWARD VIEW** of part of the Makena coast showing Makena Bay and landing (near photo bottom). The golden strand fronting the Maui Prince Hotel is Maluaka; Oneuli Beach flanks the bay beside Puu Olai.

The Village Gallery

Just south of Makena Bay is one of the island's earliest churches, **KEAWALAI** (1832). Built primarily of coral blocks from the offshore reefs, its name "calm bay" reflects the treasured sentiments of many residents. Oil painting by Maui artist George Allan.

(*center*) **MAKENA LANDING**, a tiny boat ramp along the old Makena road (seaward of Makena Alanui Road), was, until the 1920s, Maui's busiest port. It exported sugar from Ulupalakua Ranch and transported cattle to Kahoolawe, then an enormous cattle ranch. From around 1850 to 1920, Makena was a busy, thriving community supporting more than one hundred families. When Kahului Harbor was expanded, this port, along with the Kihei pier, was abandoned and finally wrecked during World War II training exercises. (*bottom*) Not every sunset on Maui is viewed through coconut palms.

Cameron Kepler

119

(*top*) **MALUAKA** is the original name of an *ahupuaa* (land-division) which included this beach and a long triangle of uplands above it. The word "Maluaka" has several translations; my favorite is: "the peace which suffuses one's soul as the moon rises." *Mauka* of this beautiful beach, also pictured on the front cover, lies the Maui Prince Hotel. (*below*) Storm clouds highlight the view of Molokini from **ONEULI BEACH**. Oneuli is tucked in a secluded bay just north of Puu Olai.

Cameron Kepler

The curving sweep of **ONELOA BEACH**, the last sizable stretch of sand for forty-three miles, is viewed from an airplane looking north and through *kiawe* from the flanks of Puu Olai en route to Little Makena Beach. Oneloa, whose Hawaiian name means "long sands," and which is also known locally as Big, Makena, or Hippie Beach, is a prime stretch of sand 3,300 feet long and over 100 feet wide hugging the southern flanks of Puu Olai. It is Maui's last undeveloped beach. Residents have struggled for years to preserve it *en toto*; the fight with private developers continues. The Oneloa area is outstanding, not only for its spectacular golden sands, but for the crystalline depths of adjacent Ahihi Bay. These waters are particularly clear because inland of the beach are some shallow ponds which collect runoff from heavy rains, thus preventing siltation of the bay. Bodysurfing here is thrilling and snorkeling is clear with a variety of fish. The southern end is best (**bottom center of photo**), but don't expect fish to be as tame as at Molokini or Keawakapu. Makena Beach is particularly known for its sister cove, the infamous Little Makena or Puu Olai Beach, reached by way of a short hike over Puu Olai's cliffs. This is Maui's unofficial nude beach. Be aware, however, that *although tanning* au naturelle *is very pleasant, it is illegal.* You may well end up in the hands of an enforcement agent.

Cameron Kepler

Bob Abraham

LAVA COASTLINE

The **AHIHI-KINAU NATURAL AREA RESERVE**, comprising 2,000 acres of jagged lava and crystalline waters, is ruggedly scenic. This rounded peninsula is a lava outcrop resulting from Maui's last volcanic eruption (1790). Its "No Fishing" regulations are strictly enforced. The reserve embraces rocky and forested lands, Hawaiian village sites, ancient fishponds, offshore waters, and three anchialine (tidal brackish) ponds. Geographically this includes Cape Kinau and adjacent portions of Ahihi Bay (northward) and La Perouse Bay (southward). Incidentally, La Perouse Bay was originally called Keoneoio Bay, after the *oio* (bonefish) which customarily gathered in its sandy bottom and which were caught in sweep nets drawn by several canoes.

From the sign (*right*) a trail leads into the reserve, where raised sections of an ancient trail are still visible. In 1786,

Cameron Kepler

explorer La Perouse recorded four fishing villages here, whose ruins are now on the state's historic register. (*below*) Ancient fishponds, which originally fattened bonefish and mullet. The feasibility idea of raising fish in these ponds by traditional methods is currently under consideration by the State of Hawaii.

(*top*) **VILLAGE SITES** on Cape Kinau. In 1786, La Perouse found their inhabitants kind and polite. (*center*) Lava **SHELTER**, still intact. (*left*) Cast-off **CRAB SHELLS** of *aama* (*Grapsus grapsus*) litter the jagged mounds of *aa* lava along this coast.

James Maragos

Limu or **SEAWEED** has always been an important and nutritious part of the Hawaiian diet, especially in areas such as Makena where wetland taro could not be cultivated. Photo shows *limu lipoa* (*Dictyopteris australis*), a green-brown limu with ruffled edges, formerly collected in quantity for supplying essential trace minerals to the traditional Hawaiian diet.

123

SNORKELING in the Ahihi-Kinau Preserve is a treat, but is not recommended for novices. The two best locations are Ahihi Cove, right where the road skirts the water's edge, and Ahihi Bay ("The Dump"), further south beside a parking lot in the lava. Park your car and walk down the small trail to a grove of *kiawe* trees. There is no beach at either place, so exercise care when traversing the ragged, sometimes slippery, rocks. Snorkel out to the rocky points or stay in the shallows. (***above and below***) **KUMU** or whitesaddle goatfish (*Parupeneus porphyreus*) and *kihikihi* or **MOORISH IDOL** (*Zanclus cornutus*).

Ann Fielding

Ed Robinson

Three **ANCHIALINE** (pron. *ann-kee-ay-line*) **POOLS,** nestled within Cape Kinau's lava flow, are unique to Hawaii. Although situated where one might expect fresh water, these pools are fed by tides through narrow subsurface channels and are thus slightly brackish. They harbor species of shrimps found nowhere else in the world and also attract occasional rare birds. Growing at the pools' edge are stands of **MAKALOA SEDGE.** These "reeds," historically associated with the island of Niihau and today uncommon elsewhere, were favored by the *alii* (Hawaiian royalty) as the choicest, most flexible mat materials in the islands. Kings arranged expeditions to Niihau to gather them. *Makaloa* mats were woven so finely they averaged ten to twelve cross-strips to the inch, a mesh equivalent to a fine machine-knitted sweater.

What a surprise to find ferns in the scorching, practically waterless coastal lava of Maui's starkest deserts!

(*above*) The **GOLD FERN** (*Pityrogramma calomelanos*), an introduced species from tropical America, leaves its imprint on a pair of jeans. The undersides of this fern's fronds are so well-covered with spores they drop off when touched. (*right*) A tiny fern, **LAUKAHI** (*Ophioglossum concinnum*), is very rare: please do not trample on, or pick it. (*bottom*) **AUHUHU** (*Tephrosia purpurea*), an ancient fish poison, is exceedingly rare. The least known of all Polynesian plant introductions into Hawaii, *auhuhu* is a legume with tiny white, pea-like flowers. Throughout the Pacific, native peoples bundled its stems and leaves, crushed and threw them into pools. Its toxic sap, which stuns fish, is not harmful to humans.

127

Maui Prince Hotel

Makena's sole hotel, the V-shaped **MAUI PRINCE**, opened in 1986, was designed to maximize ocean views for its 300 rooms and suites. Both indoors and out, this Japanese-owned, locally-managed hotel offers unmistakably foreign touches mingled with modern Hawaiian decor. Each arriving guest receives a lei, a Japanese hot *oshibori* (thick terry cloth scented with amaretto), a fresh fruit plate, chilled mineral water, and the choice of Western-style bathrobes or *ukatas* (informal cotton robes). A truly Japanese feature is the fastidious raking of the resort's crushed coral pathways and rock gardens. The hotel's luxuries include 24-hour room service, full length mirrors, large writing desks, refrigerators, babysitting, catamaran rides, etc. Wedding and honeymoon packages are specialties.

Makena also has condominiums, some presently under construction. (**below**) Beautiful Maluaka Beach affords privacy, excellent swimming and snorkeling, and stunning views.

Maui Prince Hotel

(*center*) The Hakone Japanese restaurant offers a **SUSHI BAR** with tempting rice delicacies wrapped in thin seaweed, accompanied by pickles and meticulously carved vegetables. Authentic food is prepared by a certified chef from Japan. (*bottom left*) Waterfalls, streams, Oriental stone lanterns, footbridges, carp, and tropical foliage combine elements from East and West in the spacious **COURTYARD**. This 30,000 square foot area, open to the sky, is wafted by cool ocean breezes from its sides. Its bold architectural lines are softened by native **treeferns** and **spathiphyllums** (relatives of anthuriums) which thrive within muted light. (*bottom right*) Golf and tennis receive superior national ratings.

(*above*) Each evening, a small ensemble of **CLASSICAL MUSICIANS** (strings and woodwinds) plays background music in the Maui Prince courtyard.

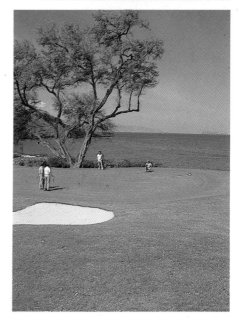

129

CHAPTER VI BEYOND MAKENA

ARCHAEOLOGICAL SITES

Makena Road ends at La Perouse Bay. DO NOT DRIVE BEYOND THE PARKING LOT. Beyond Makena, and extending for miles, is an ancient Hawaiian rocky trail. This area, even more than Makena, is not for everyone, especially people who are prone to heat headaches, unaccustomed to hiking, or who are not adequately prepared. Would-be adventurers should hike with groups such as the Sierra Club. Minimum requirements are: daypacks, leather boots, long pants, plenty of fresh water, food , aspirin, hat, sunscreen, bandaids and elastic bandages. (*opposite and below*) Around 1516, Kiha, son of Chief Piilani, completed constructing a rocky trail, the *alaloa* ("long road") around Maui's entire shoreline. Much of it has disappeared with modern road building, but one of the finest remaining portions is the original **PIILANI (KING'S) HIGHWAY**, beginning at La Perouse Bay and extending eastward across a huge expanse of unstable, jagged lava (Do not confuse this with the modern Piilani Highway, Route 31, inland of Kihei.) The *alaloa* had few turns and no bridges but people used the best available means of traversing topographical inconveniences. They swam or swung by hand-made ropes. Canoes sometimes ferried people across streams or along the shore. Along the *alaloa* trained runners (*kukini*) carried speedy messages or fresh food for the chiefs (*alii*), and people heaped their wares (*hala* mats, feathers, foodstuffs) in certain spots for the tax-collectors. Note the *ahu* (cairn) against the sky, marking the location of an ancient land division (**below, right**). The **ribbons of CASCADING LAVA** mark the location of Maui's most recent volcanic eruption around

Cameron Kepler

Carrying these smooth stepping stones inland involved "a living chain" of workers to the nearest beach.

1790. As the Hawaiians had no written language prior to the 19th century, no one recorded this event on paper, so calculating its date gave geologists some fun. Their first estimate of 1750 was based on the fact that a certain Charlie Ako's grandfather had seen the eruption when he was "a boy big enough to carry two coconuts from the beach to the upper road (around four miles and a 2,000-foot climb)!" The more accurate date was deduced, as recently as 1965, from the study of two navigator's maps. That of La Perouse (1786) indicated a broad bay in the area, whereas that of Vancouver (1793) clearly marked a rounded peninsula Split the dates and you have 1790.

Cameron Kepler

(*left, below*) When the first explorers sailed along Maui's coast, they observed numerous small villages. Today, the entire area is uninhabited, although Kanaio has been used for military targets. In those days, native forests, clothing Haleakala's slopes from sea level up to the cinders of Haleakala Crater, attracted clouds which fed watercourses and underground springs. Along the shore **evidences of FORMER HABITATION**— house sites, *heiau* (temples), canoe sheds—still remain for those willing to trek across hot, clinkery lava. Please respect them. Step *over*, rather than *on*, the stone "walls."

Cameron Kepler

Cameron Kepler

(*left*) In old Hawaii, salt was a staple item, and Maui's south shore was a prime location for its collection. Salt was added to meat, fish, vegetables and seaweeds (*limu*) for eating and preservation, and rubbed into wounds as an antiseptic. **SALT PANS**, such as these from a deserted village, assisted in the making of this sun evaporated commodity.

(*top*) This crumbling foundation of an ancient **HEIAU** at Wekea Point reminds us of a lost way of life. *Heiau*, of diverse shapes and sizes, dotted the islands. All were sacred temples where prized offerings—pigs, coconuts, and humans—were sacrificed in order to appease the gods. Some *heiau* are so ancient they are credited to the work of *menehune* (minuscule mythical people). Here, one could worship the gods of agriculture, rain and thunder, and find refuge from evil spirits or the shadow of death. Power (*mana*) drawn from them was believed to bring peace, health and prosperity.

In the early 1820s, King Kamehameha II decreed that all the ancient gods be abandoned in favor of worshipping the one true God of the missionaries. All *heiau* were to be destroyed. It is said that when one *heiau* on Oahu burned, its fiery glow was seen from Kauai, 100 miles away. Maui's sacred sites also suffered greatly; however, today some remnants have been reconstructed and/or protected. Increasing numbers of ruins are currently being added to the National Register of Historic Sites. Today, tales of spirits and ghosts from this area still live.

Early explorers had difficulty finding suitable landings along this entire **LAVA-GIRT SHORE** (*right, below*). La Perouse, in 1786, was the only one who succeeded, but two years later this pioneering explorer died during a hurricane in the southwest Pacific. Fortunately his diaries still exist, giving us an idea of 18th century life in Hawaii. *(center)* **SEA CUCUMBERS** (*Actinopyga mauritiana*) were frequently eaten by the people of old. Their Hawaiian name *loli* also means spotted. Tidepools harbor crabs, baby fish, worms, sea-urchins, eels, shells, etc.

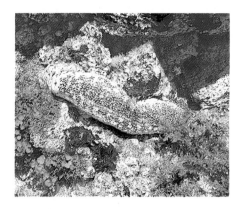

Cameron Kepler

134

(*right*) Heaped upon several inlets miles beyond La Perouse Bay lie tons of driftwood, not from the islands but from the Washington and Oregon coasts. Pictured is **LUMBERYARDS BEACH** in Kanaio, whose gravelly beaches are heavily littered with ocean-tossed cedars, pines and firs. Ocean currents toss the logs for years, focusing and eventually hurling them on a handful of beaches on Maui and Kahoolawe. This is most unusual, as Hawaiian beaches are typically devoid of debris. (*center*) **GOOSE-NECK BARNACLES** or *pioi* were evidently never worth eating; here they impart a marine flavor to a wave-worn culm of bamboo.

CHAPTER VII KAHOOLAWE

Kahoolawe—a "forbidden island" like Niihau. Once named Kanaloa, after one of the four major Hawaiian gods, it is now Kahoolawe, "Land of Gathering Driftwood."

Eons ago, so they say, Wakea the Sky Father and Haumea-papa, the Earth Mother, gave birth to all the Hawaiian Islands. Later some jealousy between two goddesses developed, and a curse (*kapu*) was placed upon the Island of Kahoolawe, declaring that "no man can love that child...anyone who takes Kahoolawe will suffer defeat." Curiously this island, the smallest of Hawaii's eight major islands (46 sq. mi.) has suffered more than any other, especially during the last 140 years: almost every shred of life, including its soil, has been blown, nibbled, or blasted away.

During the early 19th century Queen Kaahumanu banished Catholics, and later hard-core prisoners, to Kahoolawe. In 1863 sheep and goats began wreaking havoc with its native vegetation. In 1910 the entire island was proclaimed a Territorial Forest Reserve but reclamation efforts were slow, and in 1917 a key person in Kahoolawe's history, rancher Angus McPhee, initiated reforestation efforts. Within one year he had sold 13,000 goats, shot countless sick ones, planted 5000 native trees and eucalyptus windbreaks, and built several redwood tanks.

During World War II, the U.S. Navy took over Kahoolawe, and since then till 1990 countless tons of bombs have blasted its barren landscape. Concerned residents, along with the Protect Kahoolawe Ohana Association, fought for years to stop the bombing and protect archaeological sites. Their recent success is one step toward Kahoolawe's recovery.

The steep face of an offshore island, Puu Koae, and the cliffs of Kamohio Bay: a climber's view.

Only seven miles from Maui, the east end of Kahoolawe's volcanic cone breaks the horizon. Its highest points, Puu Moaulanui (1477 feet) and Puu Moaulaiki (1444 feet), impart two humps to the island's low dome. This irregular profile is a foolproof means of distinguishing Kahoolawe from Lanai, which has a higher and more uniform outline. Kahoolawe from Molokini's jagged, overhung ridgeline (**top**); Polo Beach (**center left**); atop Puu Olai (**center right**); and high above Cape Kinau (**bottom**).

Cameron Kepler

Cameron Kepler

Bob Hobdy/Department of Land & Natural Resources

Cameron Kepler

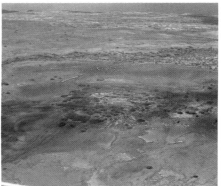

Bob Hobdy/DNLR

A century of overgrazing and bombing on Kahoolawe has been disastrous environmentally and archaeologically. (*top*) Extreme **EROSION** near Puu Moiwi (1161 feet); (*center left*) A **PIT** dubbed "sailor's cap" by the Navy, a result of a nuclear test bomb using 20,000 lbs. of TNT. (*center right*) A circular **TARGET** sits atop infertile clay at Lua Kealialalo. (*bottom*) Boulder fields atop red hardpan east of Kanaloa Gulch: virtually all the topsoil is gone from large areas. Mounds of the desert-adapted Australian **SALTBUSH** (*Atriplex semibaccata*) dot the moonlike landscape.

Cameron Kepler

Cameron Kepler

(*top*) Cliff-girt **KAMOHIO BAY** cuts deeply into Kahoolawe's south coast. (*center left*) Atop an adjacent island, Puu Koae, 376 feet high (**bottom**), sits an ancient **FISHING SHRINE** or *ko'a*, where offerings to the gods were once placed. Personal fishing gods or *aumakua* were embodied in fish such as sharks and eels. Today the site offers protection to an uncommon native succulent *Portulaca lutea* (foreground). (**center right**) One of the 171 **ARCHAEOLOGICAL SITES** now on the National Register of Historic Places.

Cameron Kepler

(*top*) Ancient Hawaiian **PETROGLYPHS** near Kanaloa Gulch. (*center*) Reforestation efforts by Hawaii State Department of Natural Resources are ongoing, but survival is low, especially for native plants. Pictured is four-year-old **TAMARISK** (*Tamarix* spp.), a hardy, drought-resistant windbreak native to the Mediterranean. (*center right*) Wildlife is sparse on Kahoolawe, but seabirds such as this **RED-TAILED TROPICBIRD** (*Phaethon rubricauda*) still nest successfully on high cliffs. (*bottom*) Picturesque **KAKA POINT** faces Maui.

Bob Hobdy/DNLR

Cameron Kepler

INDEX

INDEX

Other Titles by the Author

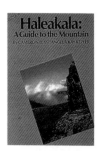

Haleakala: A Guide to the Mountain
by Cameron B. and Angela K. Kepler

The entire mountain, from sun-spangled shorelines through lush lowland forests, verdant pastures and alpine expanses. History, geography cultural events and accommodations, a complete hiking and camping guide, points of interest, day trips and extended hikes. Over 200 color photographs, maps.

ISBN 0-935180-67-2 • 96 pages • 5 3/4" X 8 1/2" • $8.95

Proteas in Hawaii
by Angela K. Kepler
Photography by Jacob R. Mau

Floral photography at its best through the lens of awardwinning, Maui-born photographer Jacob R. Mau. Over 200 photographs on this amazing flowering plant family. Dr. Kepler's authoritative text provides a wealth of information on correct English and scientific names including pronunciation, buying and caring for the plants, flower arrangements, general and historic information. The first book on proteas ever published in the United States.

ISBN 0-935180-66-4 • 80 pages • 5 3/4" X 8 1/2" • $8.95

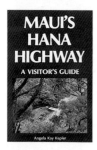

Maui's Hana Highway: A Visitor's Guide
by Angela K. Kepler

The incredible 52-mile journey of 617 curves and 56 bridges through some of Hawaii's most breathtaking scenery. Packed with hundreds of facts and interesting information.

ISBN 0-935180-67-2 • 80 pages • 5 3/4" X 8 1/2" • $8.95

Exotic Tropicals of Hawaii: Heliconias, Gingers, Anthuriums and Decorative Foliage
by Angela Kay Kepler photography by Jacob R. Mau

Tropicals furnish the ultimate in floral brilliance with their stunning beauty and long vase life. Nowhere else in the world but Hawaii can be found such a staggering variety of exotic tropical flowers. Now for the first time ever, a complete account of over 136 species of gingers, heliconias and Hawaii's other "tropicals," including anthuriums, birds-of-paradise, ornamental bananas, fanciful and "jungle foliage." Presented in lavish color accompanied by an authoritative text that includes correct English and scientific names, usage, flower arrangement.

ISBN 0-935180-83-4 • 5 3/4" X 8 1/2" • 112 pp • softcover • $9.95

HOW TO ORDER
Send check or money order with an additional $3.00 for the first book and 50 cents for each additional book to cover mailing and handling to:

Mutual Publishing
1127 11th Ave., Mezz. B
Honolulu, HI. 96816
808-732-1709 Fax 734-4094